12.95
W9-CMM-748

AUTHOR 101

BESTSELLING SECRETS FROM TOP AGENTS

The Insider's Guide to What Agents and Publishers Really Want

Rick Frishman and Robyn Freedman Spizman
with Mark Steisel

WITHDRAWN

Adams Media
Avon, Massachusetts

LONGWOOD PUBLIC LIBRARY

Copyright © 2006, FME, Inc.,
and Robyn Freedman Spizman Literary Works, LLC.
All rights reserved. This book, or parts thereof, may not be reproduced
in any form without permission from the publisher; exceptions
are made for brief excerpts used in published reviews.

AUTHOR 101 is a trademark of FME, Inc.,
and Robyn Freedman Spizman Literary Works, LLC.

Published by
Adams Media, an F+W Publications Company
57 Littlefield Street, Avon, MA 02322
www.adamsmedia.com

ISBN: 1-59337-417-8

Printed in the United States of America.

J   I   H   G   F   E   D   C   B   A

Library of Congress Cataloging-in-Publication Data
Frishman, Rick.
Author 101, bestselling secrets from top agents :
the insider's guide to what agents and publishers really want /
by Rick Frishman and Robyn Freedman Spizman with Mark Steisel.
p.   cm.
Includes index.
ISBN 1-59337-417-8
1. Authorship—Marketing. 2. Literary agents. I. Title: Author one
hundred one, bestselling secrets from top agents. II. Title: Author one
hundred and one, bestselling secrets from top agents. III. Spizman,
Robyn Freedman. IV. Steisel, Mark. V. Title.
PN161.F748 2005
808'.020688—dc22
2005026445

This publication is designed to provide accurate and authoritative information with
regard to the subject matter covered. It is sold with the understanding that the publisher is not engaged in rendering legal, accounting, or other professional advice. If
legal advice or other expert assistance is required, the services of a competent professional person should be sought.
        —From a *Declaration of Principles* jointly adopted by a Committee of the
American Bar Association and a Committee of Publishers and Associations

Many of the designations used by manufacturers and sellers to distinguish their products are claimed as trademarks. Where those designations appear in this book and
Adams Media was aware of a trademark claim, the designations have been printed
with initial capital letters.

This book is available at quantity discounts for bulk purchases.
For information, please call 1-800-872-5627.

All it takes to get a book published is getting one person to say "yes." We dedicate this book to the editors, publishers, and individuals along the way who said "yes" to us and hopefully will say "yes" to you too.

■ ■ ■

To my wife, Robbi, with love and thanks.
—*Rick Frishman*

To my husband, Willy, and our children, Justin and Ali.
You make life a bestseller!
—*Robyn Freedman Spizman*

Contents

vii   Foreword *by Peter Miller*

xi   Acknowledgments

xv   Introduction

1   *Chapter 1* ■ Agents and the Publishing Industry

11   *Chapter 2* ■ Agent ABCs: The Basics

25   *Chapter 3* ■ The Agenting Process Explained

44   *Chapter 4* ■ So Why an Agent?

53   *Chapter 5* ■ So Why Not an Agent?

60   *Chapter 6* ■ Before You Contact an Agent

81   *Chapter 7* ■ Query Letters and E-mail

95   *Chapter 8* ■ Reports from the Trenches

110   *Chapter 9* ■ Finding the Best Agent for You

123   *Chapter 10* ■ How to Interest the Right Agent

133   *Chapter 11* ■ Why Agents Love Platforms

145   *Chapter 12* ■ Rights Involved

152   *Chapter 13* ■ Author/Agent Agreements

163   *Chapter 14* ■ Leaving an Agent

169   *Chapter 15* ■ What Agents Hate

179   *Chapter 16* ■ Summing Up

187   *Appendix A* ■ Glossary of Publishing Terms

195   *Appendix B* ■ Resource Directory

215   *Appendix C* ■ The AAR Canon of Ethics

219   *Appendix D* ■ Sample Author/Agent Agreements

226   *Appendix E* ■ Publishing Contract Checklist

233   Index

Foreword

BOOKS AND PUBLISHING are my life. I've been a literary representative for thirty years, placed over 1,000 books worldwide, represented many bestsellers, and dealt with all of the top players in the publishing industry. I'm also a published author and have managed numerous motion picture and television properties. As the author of *Author! Screenwriter!* (Adams Media), I know the book business inside and out. So, I feel well qualified to say that the book you are about to read, *Author 101: Bestselling Secrets from Top Agents*, will be one of the most important investments in your writing career. In fact, the entire Author 101 series should be on every writer's bookshelf and read cover to cover!

This book arrives at the perfect time. Today, more than ever, it's hard to get published, and getting published without an agent is even tougher. You see, publishing has become a specialized, highly complex industry that is increasingly hard to crack and difficult to navigate. Whether you're an aspiring author or even if you have been previously published, you need the right agent in your corner—a professional who knows the ropes, who can guide you through the complexities of the process, push and fight for you, and help you to chart a long, successful, and fulfilling career.

Although being represented by a literary agent can be essential to your career, finding the right one isn't easy. The problem is that agents vary widely, according to their experience, areas of interest, specialties, competence, dedication, and integrity. And literary agents are not required to be licensed or certified by governmental bodies. In addition, when you hire an agent, you're looking to build a relationship, to find a partner who will be your trusted advisor, chief strategist, and close confidant throughout your career.

Finding the right literary agent takes planning, work, and dedication. It requires you to go through a precise step-by-step process that most people simply don't understand and don't know how to begin. Once you get started, it's easy to get discouraged because the route can be filled with roadblocks, detours, and dead ends that stop many writers in their tracks.

Bestselling Secrets from Top Agents will show you the way; it will give you the answers. It clearly explains exactly what you must do to find and hire the right literary agent for you. It also tells you what to avoid. This invaluable book is filled with inside secrets shared by dozens of experienced agents who take you behind the scenes and explain how agents, editors, and publishers think and how you must proceed. So gobble it all up—read, enjoy, learn, devour, and digest everything you can from this comprehensive book on the inside world of agents and how they work.

This book is special because of its authors. I've known Rick Frishman for more than twenty-five years; he is one of the most knowledgeable and respected people in the publishing PR business. Rick's firm, Planned Television Arts, has probably promoted more *New York Times* bestsellers than any other public relations firm in the business. The prolific Robyn Freedman Spizman, Rick's writing partner, is a highly acclaimed and accomplished author; co-owner of The Spizman Agency, a successful book PR firm that serves as the southeastern affiliate of Planned Television Arts; and a nationally recognized media personality. Rick and Robyn are true industry insiders and only such insiders have the kind of access to the sources and depth of information that fill this wonderful book. Together, they have created a literary bible for all authors who wish to achieve their publishing goals.

One caution: Great authors usually have terrific agents. So after you read this book, use it to find and hire the right agent, not to act as your own agent. Representing yourself can be disastrous. Over the years, I have made a lot of money for a lot of authors—some have received millions of dollars. I have also seen careers climb and then implode because authors who became successful fell prone to the old saying, "Money can provoke greed into rearing its ugly head."

When you select the right literary representation, consider it a bond, a partnership, and be prepared to run the distance—for the length of your career. This book will give you the tools to finish the race and continue to actively compete on the circuit for years to come. As your companion and coach, it will guide you toward success.

I thank Rick and Robyn for sharing this valuable information with us.

—Peter Miller, President
PMA Literary and Film Management, Inc.
www.pmalitfilm.com

Acknowledgments

WE FEEL PRIVILEGED to work with books and publishing and to have so many wonderful, dynamic, and intelligent people in our lives. They have constantly enriched our lives and we constantly count our blessings.

To begin, our warmest thanks to Gary Krebs and Scott Watrous of Adams Media, who gave us the green light when we presented this book series. Their steadfast enthusiasm for the project and encouragement has lit a fire under us. We also want to express our appreciation to our editor, Paula Munier, for her guidance and support, and to thank the staff at Adams Media.

We especially want to express our deep appreciation to Lloyd Jassin, Esq., a leading New York City literary attorney who not only helped us with the legal material in this book, but also wrote much of it. Thank you, Lloyd, for your graciousness, your generosity, and your amazing expertise.

Thanks also to our many and gifted literary contacts whose help and wisdom made this book possible. When we asked them to help us, these friends consistently came through and shared their remarkable knowledge, experience, and insights with us. They selflessly took time from their busy schedules to help us and the readers of this book.

So, to all of you who have given us so much, please accept our heartfelt thanks. We are extremely grateful for your help! We would like to especially acknowledge and thank the following people:

Andree Abecassis   Jennifer Enderlin   Sharlene Martin
Jill Alexander   Debra W. Englander   Peter Miller
Peter Applebome   Grace Freedson   John Monteleone
Ken Atchity   Don Gastwirth   Paula Munier
Harriette Bawarsky   George Greenfield   Erin Reel
Pamela Brodowsky   Marion Gropen   Jody Rein
Joanne Brownstein   Lloyd Jassin, Esq.   Diane Reverand
Sheree Bykofsky   Jeremy Katz   Janet Rosen
Leanne Chearney   Edward W. Knappman   Carol Susan Roth
Danielle Chiotti   Elaine Koster   James Schiavone, Ed. D.
June Clark   Gary Krebs   Bob Silverstein
Roger Cooper   Ronald E. Laitsch   Bonnie Solow
Richard Curtis   Michael Larsen   John Willig
Jane Dystel   Bonnie Marson

We also wish to pay homage and express our great appreciation to the book world's literary gurus, those pioneering individuals who paved the way for all of us through their outstanding efforts. These superheroes blazed the trail and showed us—and so many others—that we could fulfill our dreams of being published authors. With that said, we wish to thank Jack Canfield, Mark Victor Hansen, Jeff Herman, John Kremer, Michael Larsen, Jan Nathan, Dan Poynter, and Marilyn Ross, as well as many others, too numerous to mention, who have devoted their careers to helping aspiring authors succeed. It is with deep appreciation that we salute them for sharing their knowledge and their dedication to writing and publishing.

From Robyn: To my wonderful family—my husband, Willy, and our children, Justin and Ali. You fill my life with laughter and love. To my parents, Phyllis and Jack Freedman, who have cheered me on to success. To my brother Doug who said, "Real authors have agents." To Genie, Sam and Gena and my devoted family and wonderful group of friends. And a special thanks to the Spizman Agency, Jenny Corsey, and Bettye Storne for your unending devotion and continued support.

To my coauthor, Rick Frishman, who is genuinely one of the finest human beings on this planet. Thank you, Rick, for being such a remarkable friend and coauthor. And to the talented Mark Steisel, who is a total literary genius in our book!

Thanks also to Meredith Bernstein for her steadfast friendship and expert guidance throughout the years. To Ron and Mary Lee Laitsch for your belief in me and to Dr. Ava Wilensky for encouraging me to write a book for authors, and to my readers, who continue to grace me with their presence. I am most fortunate to have all of you in my life.

From Rick: The first thank you goes to my wonderful coauthor, Robyn Spizman, who I've known for over twenty years and is one of the finest coauthors a guy could ask for!

Mark Steisel—your help and wisdom have been invaluable. Working with you has been a joy.

Thank you to our super editor at Adams Media, Paula Munier, and to Gary Krebs and, of course, the man who made this happen, Scott Watrous. Thank you, Beth Gissinger and Gene Molter, publicity gurus at Adams, for all of your hard work.

I have to acknowledge Mike (Manny) Levine, who founded Planned Television Arts in 1962 and was my mentor, and partner, for over eighteen years. Mike taught me that work has to be fun and meaningful and then the profits will follow.

To my exceptional management team at PTA—David Hahn, David Thalberg, and Sandy Trupp—your professionalism, loyalty, and friendship mean more to me than you will ever know. To Hillary Rivman, who helped build PTA and is still an affiliate and friend of our company. To Bob Unterman—you are always there when I need you and are truly a best friend. To the staff of PTA, you are the best in the business.

Thank you to David and Peter Finn, Tony Esposito, Richard Funess, and all of my colleagues at Ruder Finn. It is an honor to be part of this amazing company.

To my friends Mark Victor Hansen and Jack Canfield. Making the journey with the two of you has been incredible, and your friendship and advice have been invaluable.

To Harvey Mackay, for the lessons about networking and for your amazing support. You are in a class of your own.

To my mother and father, for keeping me out of the fur business and helping me discover my own destiny. And to my brother Scott, who has always been there to support me in whatever I do.

To my children, Adam, Rachel, and Stephanie. Watching you grow into fine young individuals has been the highlight of my life. And to my wife, Robbi—you are my strength.

Introduction

IT'S BEEN A LONG and difficult process. You've worked like crazy, you've spent so much time to research your book, organize it, draft it, edit it, rewrite it, polish it, and polish it some more to get it ready. Now it's finished and ready to go, but where should you send it? Where do you go from here?

Your friends tell you to hire a literary agent. Agents, they say, are the best way to get your book published. But what do you do? How do you hire an agent? How do you know whom to contact? How do you contact him or her? What do you say when you reach him or her? How do agents work?

Good questions, all of them—questions that all writers should ask, because so few of them know the answers. Well, in this book, we're going to give you the answers. We're going to pass on advice from top agents, editors, and other publishing professionals to fill you in on agents from *A* to *Z*. The information in this book will arm you with numerous tools and approaches that you can use to find the best agent for you.

Getting an agent isn't easy. It seems like everybody wants to write a book and get it published. So agents are swamped with requests from would-be authors; many told us that they get hundreds of inquiries each week. To handle the onslaught, agents have created procedures and protocols that aspiring writers must follow if they want to work with them. Agents spend much of their time screening writers' submissions, and they accept only a few.

As experienced writers, we've been where you are. We know what it's like. So, to write this book, we interviewed dozens of agents. We asked them point-blank to share their secrets, to give us information on the nuts and bolts of what writers should do.

We found out that when you approach literary agents, it's essential to be prepared. It's important to have done a lot of homework and learned beforehand what agents do, what they want, and what you have the right to expect from them. Similarly, it's important for them to know your expectations. When you and your agent know each other's expectations, this promotes good communication and helps ensure that you're both on the same page.

Agents are professionals, busy professionals, so they insist on dealing with only informed clients. Frankly, most agents simply don't have the time to explain the facts of publishing life to aspiring writers; they have far too much to do. So they expect writers to be well informed and well prepared when they contact them. Being so informed can start the client/agent relationship on a more efficient and productive level . . . and it may be the only way you can get in the door.

This book applies mainly to nonfiction writers, but fiction writers will also gain a great deal from it because much of the information that we provide about securing an agent applies to all authors. Whatever kind of book you plan to write—nonfiction, fiction, poetry, children's, academic, and so on—be sure to conduct specific research on agents who handle your type of book and their specific submission requirements.

Please feel free to contact us about this book or to send us your comments and questions at *www.author101.com.*

Enjoy this book as well as your journey to becoming a published author; it's a fabulous club to join. And as you navigate through the publishing process, at all stages, try to help other aspiring authors. Pass the torch, and explain to them the lessons you learned from reading this book and from your efforts to get your book published.

—Rick Frishman and Robyn Freedman Spizman

CHAPTER 1

"I'm all in favor of keeping dangerous weapons out of the hands of fools.
Let's start with typewriters."
Frank Lloyd Wright

Agents and the Publishing Industry

THIS CHAPTER WILL COVER:

► Why agents?
► Publishing is a business
► The economic climate
► Industry structure
► How agents work

"I'M BASICALLY LIKE a guy in a stream up in Alaska panning for gold. Every now and then, when I'm in that stream, I find a nugget," agent Peter Miller, founder of PMA Literary and Film Management, Inc., says.

Literary agents like Miller live to unearth nuggets. They sift through tons of queries, phone calls, and proposals looking for writing that may turn out to be pure gold. "We read everything," Miller, the author of *Author! Screenwriter!* (Adams Media), adds. "We get phone calls, e-mail queries, letter queries, proposals, screenplays, 800-page manuscripts, and gifts."

When they find those nuggets, good agents know exactly what to do. They know exactly how to steer them through the labyrinths of publishing, where so many writing projects get hopelessly lost, and bring them all the way to the bestseller list.

Working as a literary agent can be complex, difficult, and demanding. Agents serve as the gatekeepers to publishing houses; they hold the keys to a magic kingdom that writers are clamoring to enter. Agents must:

- Constantly read queries, proposals, and manuscripts; judge their merit and determine if they and their authors are marketable.
- Keep up with developments and changes in the industry.
- Review, edit, and, frequently, rewrite book proposals.
- Select editors and publishers to send proposals to.
- Field offers and negotiate contract terms and conditions.
- Counsel and advise their authors.
- Distribute royalties, monitor publishers' compliance, and find subsidiary sales opportunities.

In other words, literary agents must wear many hats.

Why Agents?

If you want to get your book published, especially with a large publisher, your best bet is to hire an agent. Many publishers will not accept unsolicited or unagented inquiries, so having your proposals and manuscripts represented by an agent may be your only opportunity to get in the door.

Agents know the publishing industry and how it works. They have long-standing relationships with editors and publishing companies, and they work continually to maintain them. They know when editors move, where they go, and who, if anyone, replaces them.

Agents know what's on editors' lists, what publishers like, and what they need. They also know the who, what, when, where, and how of approaching editors and publishing companies.

Publishers and agents have an interlocking and mutually beneficial relationship. Publishers use agents to bring them new properties. Over 80 percent of the books publishers sell are brought to them by agents. Publishers also use agents as screeners, to examine potential new projects and send them only those that the agents think will succeed.

Agents excel at learning and keeping abreast of the interests of individual publishers and feeding them what they need.

"Editors receive a shopping cart of proposals each day," New Jersey agent John Willig, of Literary Services, Inc., points out. "The value of working with an agent is that agents have reputation, access, and can get to the right editors and publishers."

Agents earn their living by selling to publishers. Since agents work on commission, they're paid only when their clients' books are sold. Therefore, agents are basically controlled by the needs and desires of their primary customers, publishers. This means they must be focused, selective, and highly tuned in to the marketplace. For every ten calls they take from writers in pursuit of an agent, less than one becomes a client.

Selling a book can be a difficult, time-consuming process, so agents must be discriminating in determining which clients to represent. They can't afford to waste their efforts on writers whose books publishers can't sell.

"An agent is effectively a vendor. He or she usually has already worked on the proposal, which gives me quality control and a partner in the creation of the book," Jeremy Katz, executive editor at Rodale Books, notes. "The author isn't really my partner until I buy the book, but I'm in business with the agent."

It's a Business!

Before we go too deeply into our discussion of agents and the roles they play, let's back up a bit and give you a brief overview of the publishing world and how it works, and let's fill you in on the present publishing climate. If you want to get your book published, it's vital for you to understand how the industry operates, the conditions that prevail, and the rules of the game you hope to play.

To most outsiders, the book-publishing industry has an aura of glamour and mystery, and publishing insiders have gone to great lengths to preserve those beliefs. The perception of glamour helps the industry get a steady stream of writers who compete to see their books in print. Writing is the industry's prime resource, and it's never been in short supply.

The mystery surrounding the industry allows publishing companies to control writers and agents. It lets them write and rewrite rules that govern the industry—rules that are written in their language, that further their goals, and that writers and agents must follow.

As a result, few outsiders know much about the publishing business and how it works. So, when unagented writers deal with publishers, they're out of their league; they don't know what to do or how and when to do it. That's where agents come in.

Literary agents are the ultimate insiders. Although they operate separate and independent businesses, they are partners with both writers and publishers. They know both sides of the story.

Agents understand the hopes and dreams of writers and how much their books mean to them. However, they also know that book publishing is a business—a big, profit-driven business. They know that publishers must make money in order to survive and that virtually every major decision in publishing reflects a business- and profit-oriented goal. And they know how to operate and represent authors in that arena.

If you are a writer who hopes to be published, you must understand the economic climate in the industry and shape your work in terms of those realities.

The Economic Climate

Over the last decade, the book publishing industry has changed dramatically. First, it experienced major consolidation. Not long ago, the industry featured dozens of large publishing houses, many of which were household names. Now, six giant companies owned by huge, multinational conglomerates dominate publishing.

The Big Six publishers—Random House, Penguin, HarperCollins, Holtzbrinck, Time Warner, and Simon & Schuster—put out about 80 percent of all books sold. For more detailed information on these companies and the imprints they publish, see our book *Author 101: Bestselling Book Proposals.*

In addition to the top six publishers, about 3,000 to 4,000 medium-sized publishers exist, along with more than 85,000 small publishers and self-publishers. With the explosion in electronic books, printing on demand and other innovations, the field continues to expand.

"The number of books that actually earn out their advance is progressively decreasing in the industry," agent Edward Knappman of New England Publishing Associates tells us. "This is attributable to the publishers' emphasis on just the top-of-the-list bestsellers, which has undercut midlist books. The large book chains are constantly flexing their muscles with publishers to get extra discounts for displays, so it's gotten like a grocery store where you pay for shelf space and product placement. Publishers don't pay for shelf space for midlist books."

Industry consolidation has changed publishing both internally and externally. Internally, corporate business methods and goals have replaced looser, more paternalistic operations. Everything is bottom-line oriented. Now, even respected editors who have produced huge megahits and international bestsellers still have to go through editorial boards, several bosses, and months of deliberation to bid on books they believe in deeply.

Externally, industry consolidation has reduced the number of publishers who buy books, which makes it harder for writers to get their books sold. Publishers that were formerly separate companies may now be owned by the same parent company. In some organizations, acquisition decisions for different imprints are made by the same people or editorial boards. So if your proposal is rejected by one imprint, it won't be purchased by that imprint's sister company.

Literary agents know such information. They know who to submit proposals to and when to make those submissions. They know what specific houses want and when they need it.

In addition, the publishing economy has changed. "In the past three years, the market has become incredibly tight and the market is running scared," according to literary manager Ken Atchity, cofounder of Los Angeles's AEI On Line. "Editors are worried about their jobs. They're being judged per title, on the success of each book. Everyone is focused on the sure thing, which is the recycling of the old brands that are already there. Anyone who has a brand name is being recycled to death, until literally they burn out. Even after they die, publishers keep publishing them. They have someone take over their name and rewrite it. The corporations that own the publishing houses are in love with brands and that's what they decided is the only way to publish."

Legendary New York City literary agent Richard Curtis, of Richard Curtis Associates, Inc., echoes Atchity's sentiments. He says, "The publishing industry has become more and more a business driven by hits. It's like music, movies, and the media; it's more and more a business for stars. People who want to enter are finding the bar has been raised higher and higher and their options are more limited."

Writers who hope to be published, especially first-time writers, must learn how to operate in today's publishing climate. Agents can show them the way.

Some Publishing Facts

According to estimates, more than 170,000 books were published in 2004, 60,000 alone in the third quarter of the year. That's a lot of books and a lot of competition! It's competition for you as an author to get your book published and sold to readers, and competition for publishers to distinguish their books.

Industry figures indicate that 80 percent of the books that are published fail. In addition, 1 percent of all books sold account for 50 percent of all publishing company profits. It takes large publishing houses a year to two years to put out a book, and the average cost is $50,000 per title.

Industry Structure

Many publishers say that they only accept submissions brought to them by agents. However, they may occasionally break that rule for a good

Rick Says

"Agented submissions get more attention. Some editors will read anything submitted by certain agents. Most editors know that agents screen submissions. Editors rely on agents because they are usually experienced, and they know quality and what sells. Agents usually won't try to interest publishers in weak material, except when it's written by a big celebrity.

"Agents often have a feel for the pulse of the industry. They're great at noticing trends early and usually can sense what will be hot. Agents are often accomplished talent spotters, and they know what particular publishing companies and/or editors want and like."

unsolicited or unagented book—if they ever hear about it, which they probably won't.

Unsolicited and unagented submissions are usually routed to the slush pile, where they will be read (maybe) by some tired, overworked junior editor. Although some mavericks may slip through, your chances of being published are far greater when a literary agent submits your work.

How Agents Work

Legally, agents represent authors; they are their client-writers' sales representatives. When publishers pay authors for advances and royalties, they send the checks to the agents, who deduct their fees and expenses and remit the balance to their clients.

Since some agents tend to work with the same publishers or editors, they can become beholden to them. This can create delicate situations, as agents must balance the interests of two, often conflicting, parties: authors and publishers.

An agent's primary job is to represent the writer and protect his or her interests. This usually involves selling the book and negotiating the contract and fees. A number of agents have expanded that role and become literary managers. Instead of just selling writers' books, these agents manage their careers and help build them into brands.

The work of a good agent continues long after the ink on the contract has dried. A good agent:

- Monitors the publisher's actions, making sure that it is keeping its bargains and putting forth its best efforts to promote and distribute the agent's clients' books.
- Watches for future opportunities and pushes for follow-up books, additional printing runs, added publicity, and other benefits.

For most writers, getting a literary agent isn't easy. Since agents don't make money unless they sell books, they're selective about the clients they take on. You can increase your chances of getting an agent by understanding the process from the agent's perspective and following his or her protocols.

Robyn Says

"Personally, I think finding a great agent is like striking gold. I'm a huge fan of the role agents can play. If you're fortunate enough to find someone who will represent you with integrity and passion, you're one lucky writer. What impresses me most about my nonfiction agent Meredith Bernstein is her passion and love of great ideas. She is extremely selective and has taught me a great deal about being an author. She has served as a very important individual in my literary career. A really dedicated agent is the best advocate your books will ever have and can keep you reaching for new literary heights."

"An agent can't tell a writer how to have the life experience or the fictional idea that will get his attention; that's up to the author," Richard Curtis points out. "An author has to have talent, if not genius, and if he or she does, it will find its way. Talent will out."

Publishing professionals know all the industry players, the shortcuts and the land mines. They are fluent in the industry language. From the first moment you attempt to do business with publishers, you're operating on their turf and speaking in their language, which is why you need an agent.

In the publishing business, the playing field isn't level; it tilts in the publishers' direction. Publishers have most of the power because they're willing to finance books and distribute books. Publishers are also full-time players; unlike many writers, publishing is their sole business, the only thing they do.

Although agents can't level the field, they can lessen the gap because they are also full-time industry professionals. Good agents know the markets, the trends and developments, and they're hardwired into the industry. They have close contacts and long-standing, trusting, and mutually beneficial relationships.

When disputes arise, agents can get involved to protect their authors and restore good working relationships. However, for many agents, their relationship with a publisher is more important than their duties, or at least their clients' perception of their duties, to their authors. This can leave authors feeling abandoned and betrayed.

Action Steps

1. List three advantages of hiring a literary agent.
2. What percentage of all books does the Big Six sell?
3. Describe the ways that you can shape your book to make it more commercially viable for a publisher.
4. What usually happens when unsolicited and unagented submissions are sent to publishing companies?
5. After a book deal is signed, how can an agent help his or her client?

Remember:

 Literary agents are the ultimate publishing industry insiders. Many publishers claim that they accept only proposals submitted by agents. Agents bring publishers over 80 percent of the books they release. Publishers also use agents as screeners to examine potential new projects and submit only those that the agents think will succeed.

 Agents are paid when their clients' books are sold. Therefore, they are basically controlled by the needs and desires of their primary customers, publishers. So, they must be focused, selective, and highly tuned in to the marketplace. For every ten calls they take from writers in pursuit of an agent, less than one becomes a client. In the next chapter, we will explain how agents work.

CHAPTER

2

"Agents do lunch, not contracts."
Alex Kozinski, Judge U.S. Court of Appeals

Agent ABCs: The Basics

THIS CHAPTER WILL COVER:

► How agents work
► Payment
► Reading fees
► AAR Canon of Ethics
► Agents or lawyers?

LITERARY AGENTS FILL two primary, and often overlapping, roles. They serve as both their clients'

1. Sales representatives
2. Literary advisors

In order to sell their clients' work, agents read it, assess it, and advise clients on its quality and market potential. They also create strategies for its sale for publication.

Agents identify potential publishers and offer their clients' writing to publishers, negotiate publishing contracts, and monitor publishers' contract compliance. Good agents constantly position their clients and work with publishers and the media to build their clients' careers.

"My agent, Esther Newberg, does three very important things," Peter Applebome, the author of *Dixie Rising: How the South is Shaping*

American Values, Politics and Culture, and *Scout's Honor: A Father's Unlikely Foray into the Woods,* says. "She works like a dog to get you the best deal. She reads your proposal and every draft you send her very quickly and gives you honest feedback. And she never lies to you. If the book isn't selling, the publisher isn't going to promote it, the book idea isn't good or the proposal is flat, she'll always tell you. You need an agent willing to give you bad news."

Agents' Compensation

As compensation for their services, agents receive a percentage of the gross income from the publishing agreements that the agents obtained. They essentially function as commission salespersons who act as middlemen or vendors to sell their clients' writing to publishers.

"Agents make an investment decision as to the return on their time as do publishers with regard to their publication of books," New Jersey agent John Willig explains. "It's all about the return and the money they can make."

What does this mean to you?

At present, the standard percentage for literary agents is 15 percent of all income that authors receive from the sale of the book and its subsidiary rights. Unless otherwise stated, this amount is calculated on gross sales on the book's cover price. Agents also usually receive 20 percent on foreign sales, and some are getting more. They receive more for foreign sales because they have to coagent with colleagues abroad.

Reasonable and Unreasonable Charges

Many literary agencies also charge for certain expenses such as photocopying, postage, and long-distance telephone calls, which are reasonable. However, some may charge for marketing, travel, and administrative expenses, which can be expensive.

Reasonable expenses that you should expect to pay are those that your agent must lay out to represent you and submit your work to publishers. The expenses you are charged should be the same that all of your agent's other clients pay.

Before you sign with an agent, get a list of all the expenses you will be charged and try to get an idea of how much they should run. Make sure that you truly understand the nature of each specific expense that you will be asked to pay. Here's a good tip: When you negotiate a contract for an agent to represent you, insist on a provision that gives you the right to approve all expenditures over a stated sum, say $50.

Unless unusual circumstances exist, you should not agree to pay for ordinary phone calls and other basic administrative expenses. If a provision is included in the contract that requires you to pay a percentage of the funds you receive for office, administrative, or managerial expenses, think twice, because those tasks are normally part of the agent's job. If the agent insists, put a dollar cap on those expenses. And whenever your agent requests or deducts expenses, request an itemized statement of those costs.

Contracting with an Agent

At a certain point, most agents will insist that you give them the exclusive rights to sell your writing; they will ask you to sign an author/agent agreement. This point varies from agent to agent, but many won't give you much of their time until you sign. Some agents don't require their clients to sign contracts. Agent Don Gastwirth, of Don Gastwirth and Associates in New Haven, Connecticut, doesn't have written agreements with many of his clients: "There are no loopholes in a handshake," Gastwirth says. "If a person ever feels unhappy with his representation, he should be free to leave at a moment's notice. A binding contract over a period of time smacks too much of indentured servitude. The minute we no longer see eye-to-eye, I want him to find an agent he's comfortable with, whom he sees eye-to-eye with."

Your agreement with an agent should specify that it applies only to a particular book or project. It should not extend to all of your writing or anything that you will ever write. It may contain an option for your next book. If you create spin-offs or new, revised, or updated versions of the agented book, the agent who negotiated the original deal will be entitled to share in revenues received.

Receiving Payment Through Agents

When publishers pay royalties, they send the checks to their writers' agents. After examining the statements to make sure that they're accurate, agents deduct the amount of their fees and expenses before they forward the authors' share to their clients. This means that on your book, your agent actually will get paid before you do.

Although agents have a fiduciary relationship with their clients and are responsible for monies received on their clients' behalf, agents are not required to be licensed or certified. The Association of Authors' Representatives (AAR), the leading agents' industry organization, has a Canon of Ethics, which sets out the ethical and business standards its members agree to follow. However, AAR does not have the power to regulate the commissions, fees, services, or other competitive practices of its members.

In addition, there are no firm rules on how quickly an agent should remit payments to clients. The AAR Canon states that payments over $50 should be sent within ten days of the date when the publisher's check clears, but the canon is an unenforceable guideline.

Literary agents are not policed or subject to disciplinary action by their peers. No professional bodies police agents as they do other professionals. An agent cannot be decertified, disbarred, or otherwise sanctioned by groups of his or her peers. The only recourse disgruntled clients have against agents is through the courts, which can be long, expensive, and exhausting. And while legal proceedings are pending, the agent can continue on merrily practicing, representing clients, and selling books.

Robyn Says

"Publishers usually pay royalties twice a year, on the first day of April and October, but the dates can vary from house to house. Royalty payments are sent to authors' agents with royalty statements.

"Shortly after receipt from the publisher, your agent should send you a copy of all royalty statements and communications regarding your book and subsidiary rights' sales. Usually, agents wait until the publisher's check has cleared, then they deduct their fee and expenses (if there are any that you have agreed to) and remit your share to you.

"If you don't completely understand *everything*—each and every breakdown, all the discounts, and how the agent calculated his or her fee—call the agent for an explanation. Set up and keep files for all your royalty statements and communications regarding income from your book."

More about AAR

AAR is a not-for-profit organization made up of independent literary and dramatic agents. It has approximately 350 members nationwide. AAR informs agents about conditions in the publishing, theater, motion picture, and television industries and in related fields. It also works to encourage cooperation among literary organizations and assists agents in representing their clients' interests.

To become a member, an applicant's primary professional activity for two years prior to applying for membership must have been as an authors' or playwrights' representative. During the eighteen-month period before applying for membership, an applicant must have been the agent principally responsible for selling the rights to ten different literary properties.

Check the agent guidebooks or agents' Web sites to find out if they are AAR members. Although membership in AAR is an indication that an agent is reputable, many reputable agents have elected not to become members. So the lack of AAR membership should not be interpreted as a sign that the agent is not on the up–and–up.

Reading Fees

Charging reading fees traditionally was a part of the literary agency business; in fact, it was a significant source of income for many agents. However, the practice has now fallen into disfavor because it was so riddled with abuses. Some agents who charged reading fees gave brief, superficial, and unhelpful critiques, if they gave any at all. Sometimes, they just took the money and ran.

In many cases, agents required writers to pay the reading fee before they would consider the writers' work. Essentially, this amounted to a fee that writers had to pay before the agents took them on as clients. All too often, the writers paid up and got little or nothing in return.

Therefore, AAR decided to prohibit its members from charging clients or potential clients for reading and evaluating literary work. And they prohibit fees even if the agency provides an extensive critique.

Although upfront fees to agents are frowned on, some agents still charge evaluation, submission, or critique fees. These fees are charged for agents to analyze writers' submissions and suggest how they can be improved. AAR prohibits these fees as well because they, too, can so easily be abused.

Agents who charge evaluation or critique fees justify them on the grounds that since they receive so many submissions, it's not financially viable to read them without being compensated. Legitimate evaluations can provide substantial benefits to writers when an experienced professional conscientiously reviews, evaluates, and critiques their writing. However, before agreeing to pay these fees, check out the agency and contact some if its clients to discuss the benefits they produced.

In lieu of evaluating and critiquing writers' submissions in-house, some literary agencies refer writers to independent editors and book doctors. While abuses have also occurred in these areas, many of these services can be extremely helpful and instructive. Again, check up on any of these referral sources as well as the agencies before you hire them.

Editors & Preditors (at *www.anotherealm.com/prededitors*) provides an online searchable directory that notes agencies that charge reading fees and have conflicts. It states when agents are recommended and not recommended.

Writer Beware (*www.sfwa.org/beware*) is a Web site that maintains information on literary agents, book doctors, subsidy publishers, and others who engage in questionable practices.

Agent Research & Evaluation *(www.agentresearch.com)* has a free agent verification service that will confirm that an agent has established a public record, and also whether it has received negative reports on the agent's business practices.

The AAR Canon of Ethics

Although the AAR Canon of Ethics may not be legally enforceable, it provides the standard of conduct that industry's most prominent association recommends. Essentially, the Canon of Ethics operates as guidelines and sets the level of conduct that you should expect when you deal with a literary agent.

Before you even start looking for an agent, educate yourself. Read the AAR's Canon of Ethics to get an idea of the level of service that agents should provide. As you read, make sure you understand each point and write down all of your questions. When you speak with agents regarding representation, ask them to answer those questions and specifically find out if they are members of AAR.

Under the canon, AAR members agree:

- To perform their professional activities according to the highest standard of conduct.
- To loyally serve their clients' business and artistic needs and not allow conflicts of interest to interfere with their services.

- To not mislead, deceive, dupe, defraud, or victimize their clients, AAR members, the general public, or anyone with whom they do business as AAR members.
- To protect the security and integrity of their clients' funds, they will:
  - Maintain separate bank accounts for money due to their clients and not commingle their clients' funds with their funds.
  - Promptly deposit funds received for clients upon receipt.
  - Promptly pay domestic earnings to clients no later than ten business days after clearance.
  - Pay foreign rights' revenues over $50 to clients within ten business days after clearance. Pay revenues under $50 a reasonable time after clearance.
  - Send payments on stock and similar rights, statements of royalties, and payments no later than the month following receipt. Each statement and payment will cover all royalties received by the twenty-fifth day of the previous calendar month. Payments for amateur rights will be made at least every six months.
- To keep each client's books of account open to that client at all times.
- To immediately advise each client in writing on the agent's receipt of a written claim that funds are due to the client. If the agent determines that the claim is so serious that the funds should not be remitted to the client, the agent will:
  - Deposit the funds in a segregated interest-bearing account for up to ninety days pending resolution of the dispute.
  - If, after ninety days, the dispute is not resolved and no agreement with the client regarding the disposition of the disputed funds has been reached, the funds will be deposited in court and notice will be given to the claimants to let them present their claims to the funds to the court. By depositing the funds, the agent's obligations under the Canon of Ethics will be fulfilled.

- That, in addition to the compensation for services agreed on by the parties, the agent may, with the client's consent, bill the client for charges incurred on the client's behalf for services such as copyright fees, manuscript retyping, photocopying, copying books to sell other rights, long-distance phone calls, and special messenger fees.
- To keep each client informed about matters entrusted to the agent and to promptly provide information the client reasonably requests.
- To not represent both buyer and seller in the same transaction. To not accept compensation or payment from the acquirer of a client's property rights, including, but not limited to, "packaging fees." Any compensation to the agent must be derived solely from the agent's client.
- That an agent may receive a "packaging fee" from the acquirer of television rights for a property owned or controlled by a client if the agent simultaneously:
  - Promptly and fully informs the client that the member may be offered a "packaging fee," which the member may decide to accept;
  - Delivers to the client a copy of AAR's statement regarding packaging and packaging fees; and
  - Gives the client the opportunity to arrange for other representation in the transaction. In no event may the agent receive both a packaging fee and compensation from the client from the transaction.
- To not receive secret profits connected with any transaction involving a client. If such a profit is received, the agent must promptly pay the client the entire amount.
- To not solicit or accept any payment or thing of value in connection with the referral of any author to a third party for any purpose. However, arrangements made with a third party in connection with the disposition of rights the agent may have in the work of the client are excepted.

- To keep their clients' financial affairs private and confidential, except for information customarily disclosed when placing rights, as required by law, or for other purposes agreed to by the client.
- To not charge clients or potential clients for reading and evaluating literary works including outlines, proposals, and partial or completed manuscripts. Agents also may not benefit when another person or entity charges for such services. The term "charge" includes any request for payment that does not cover the actual cost of returning materials. Agents may not provide consultations at conferences or other events if writers are charged separately for individual consultations with agents in which the writer's work is read or evaluated. However, agents may accept honoraria and/or reimbursement of their expenses for participating in such conferences or other events.

The full text of the AAR Canon of Ethics is provided in Appendix C of this book. We are grateful to AAR for allowing us to reproduce it here.

The Long Haul

Some agents take what New York City cab drivers call the "meter drop" approach by piling up a bunch of quick fares (book sales) rather than taking on passengers who want long rides that could build the meter (writers' careers). Try to hook up with an agent who prefers long rides to quickies.

Publishing attorneys can look after your legal and business interests in ways that literary agents cannot. Although agents can be good at contracts, attorneys are trained to understand the intricacies and nuances of contracts and literary attorneys have special, in-depth knowledge of publishing-related agreements and how the courts interpret them. Unlike agents, attorneys have rules of professional responsibility and are subject to professional disciplinary proceedings.

Literary attorneys can be outstanding negotiators and experts at publishing contracts. "If you enter into a bad publishing contract, it could be around for a very long time," cautions New York City literary attorney Lloyd Jassin. "It could haunt you, your children and your children's children because publishing contracts run for the copyright term, which is the life of the author plus seventy years."

Agents or Lawyers?

If you can afford one, a lawyer can be an important member of your literary team. While an agent's job is to make contracts on your behalf, an attorney's job is to make them better. Some agents may try to dissuade you from showing your publishing contract to an attorney, but many will embrace the chance to work with a competent professional who can improve on the terms of the deal. Plus, it's often helpful to have an official "bad guy."

Conflicts of Interest

Since agents have relationships with both the authors they represent and publishing companies, conflicts of interest can arise. For some agents, it may be more important to be on friendly terms with editors and publishers than for them to be in solidly with an author/client who is not a superstar. So, the degree of attention that those agents devote to negotiating publishing contracts may vary depending on the nature of the book, the stature of the author, and their relationship with editors and publishers.

Your agent has a direct financial interest in seeing that your book deal is completed, which can be both good and bad. While most reputable agents won't let their own financial self-interest get in the way of their advice to you, ultimately, their allegiance may be to the publisher, not you. As George Bernard cynically cracked, "The agent's real role is to procure books for publishers, not to procure publishers for authors."

Selecting a Publishing Attorney

Publishing attorneys, like literary agents, are specialists. Don't use a friend or a relative to negotiate your book contract; find a specialist, because otherwise, the negotiation could go badly. Some other guidelines to follow:

- If you hire an entertainment or copyright attorney, make sure that he or she has experience in representing authors and books. Ask what percentage of his or her practice is devoted to books and authors.
- Choose someone with an intimate knowledge of publishing. Publishing contracts are traps for unwary lawyers as well as unsuspecting authors.

Don't bother looking for a literary attorney in the Yellow Pages. You won't find one there. Literary law is a highly specialized area and publishing attorneys belong to a small club. Author or publisher groups can be good sources of referrals. The best publishing attorneys have usually worked in publishing in some capacity. Google or Yahoo! the attorney's name to find out more about his or her practice, what he or she has written, and what's been written about him or her.

Publishing attorneys tend to be clustered in major cities and their services can be expensive. Attorneys generally charge on an hourly basis, not on a percentage of what you make. Rates typically range from $250 to $450 or more. If you don't have an agent but have been offered a book contract, it makes sense to have an attorney negotiate the sale of rights on an hourly basis or for a percentage that is less than 15 percent.

Although attorneys' hourly rates can be steep, they will usually cost you far less than what you would pay an agent over the life of your book. Here's the math: 15 percent of $15,000 (a typical advance for a midlist book) is $2,250, about twice what many attorneys will charge for a full contract review and a comment letter.

Working with a Publishing Attorney

Make certain to tell your attorney your primary objectives in entering into the contract. Give your attorney a copy of your proposal; it will help him or her spot issues. For example, if you plan to publish articles or papers on the same topic as the book, your attorney will have to pay particular attention to the noncompetition clause.

When authors who have businesses write books, they are often extensions of their business. They should think about being represented by an attorney because legal issues can arise that go beyond the territory agents usually cover.

For example, if the title of the book is tied to the author's branding strategy, the author needs to be able to approve the book's ultimate title. Unless you negotiate for title approval, the publisher, not the author, has the sole right to select or change the title.

"In these situations, you're talking about brand extension," attorney Jassin advises. "Sometimes it's not about the book, it's about the author's nine-to-five career. So, you may be negotiating something more than just a book contract."

Before signing a book contract, your attorney can explain the:

- Grant of rights clause
- Option and right of first refusal
- Publisher's duty to publish
- Reversion of rights clause
- Noncompetition provision
- Postcontract liability

Some agents, such as Don Gastwirth, are both agents and attorneys. So with agent/attorneys, you can have the best of both worlds.

In most dealings with traditional publishers, an agent is usually preferable to an attorney who does not specialize in literary and publishing law. If you decide to hire an attorney, hire one who has

"A scenario that many top authors have successfully employed is hiring both an agent and a lawyer who is a literary and publishing specialist. The agents sell the authors' books, serve as their literary advisors, and manage their writing careers, and the lawyers handle their publishing contracts."

experience in literary and publishing law and performing the precise type of work you want him or her to handle.

Action Steps

1. Explain the investment decision that literary agents must make.
2. State how agents are compensated and the going rates.
3. What is AAR and what does it do?
4. What is AAR's position on agents' charging reading and similar fees?
5. List three reasons why an author would hire an agent to represent him or her rather than a literary attorney.

Remember:

 Literary agents act as both their clients' sales representatives and literary advisors. To sell their clients' work, agents read it, assess it, and advise clients on its quality and market potential. They also create strategies for its sale for publication.

 When publishers pay royalties, they send the checks to the writers' agents. After examining the statements to make sure that they're accurate, agents deduct the amount of their fees and expenses before they forward the authors' share to their clients. So on your book, your agent actually will be paid before you.

CHAPTER

3

"There are three rules for writing the novel. Unfortunately, no one knows what they are."
W. Somerset Maugham

The Agenting Process Explained

THIS CHAPTER WILL COVER:

▶ Initial contacts
▶ Query review
▶ Proposals
▶ Matchmaking
▶ Submission
▶ Negotiation
▶ Postcontract

EVERY LITERARY AGENT and agency operates somewhat differently; they may have a different emphasis, style, or approach, but all follow a basically similar pattern. Some agencies may specialize in building and managing their clients' careers, while others concentrate on making individual books into giant, blockbuster hits.

However, when it comes to selling books, agencies take similar paths. In this chapter, we're going to walk you down that path and describe the general steps involved when agents sell books.

Most writers initially contact agents via e-mail. Agents like e-mail inquiries because they're easy to answer. Responding by e-mail saves time, which is critical because most of the queries they receive are about books that the agents don't handle or are not interested in handling.

A declining number of holdouts prefer to receive query letters sent via postal mail, but they're in the minority. So check each agent's Web site to see if it states how the agent prefers to be queried.

Potential clients can also initially contact agents at conferences and other events. For information on writers' conferences, see *Writer's Digest* (*www.writersdigest.com*) and ShawGuides (*http://writing.shawguides.com*).

Many agents won't accept unsolicited telephone queries, and if you call, their screeners generally won't put you through. So, again, before you contact agents, check their Web sites to see how they wish to be approached. If, however, you do get through, most agents will ask you to submit something in writing: a query letter, a book proposal, or your entire manuscript, if it's written. Agents want written submissions so they can get a sense of the writers' ability to express themselves clearly. Written submissions also let agents see how well writers are organized and their skill in presenting themselves and their ideas.

Agents get a lot of their new clients through referrals from their existing clients and their publishing contacts. According to agent June Clark of New York's Peter Rubie Literary Agency, Ltd., it carries more weight when a new client is recommended by one of her existing clients or a close contact. Out of respect for her relationships, she will also pay more attention to these inquiries and give them more of her time.

"It's a relationship business," Clark says. "My authors know me and my tastes, so they are more likely to recommend those who'll make good matches."

The content and format for initial queries will be covered in detail in Chapter 7, "Query Letters and E-Mail."

Think Like an Agent!

So you're looking for an agent. Where are you going to find one? First of all, ask yourself this simple question: Where do agents go? To be more specific:

- ■ What conferences do they attend?
- ■ Where do they speak?
- ■ What organizations do they belong to?

Although we certainly aren't suggesting that you follow them around, we do want you to start thinking like agents think. If you do, it will improve your chances of being at the right place at the right time.

Research the literary and publishing scene in your local area. See if, when, and where any writers' associations, publishers' groups, and literary clubs meet. Are any nearby bookstores, libraries, or cafés conducting

Robyn Says

"For over two decades, I've written many nonfiction books, but I always wanted to write a children's novel. Although my agent didn't handle children's books, I couldn't get one kid's book idea out of my head.

"I attended a panel discussion in Atlanta for journalists who wanted to write books. As luck would have it, an agent, Ron Laitsch of Authentic Creations, was on the panel, and he happened to handle children's books. So after the event, I spoke with Ron about my idea. I had my pitch down pat and took the risk.

"Ironically, the book idea was about an agent. Except the agent was a kid named Kyle, who was the son of a struggling writer who couldn't sell his book. Kyle's parents were separating, and he thought that if his dad sold his book, his folks would stay together. So, he secretly posed as an agent to represent his dad's book. Kyle swore the neighborhood kids in as secret agents and plotted how to break into the publishing world.

"Ron adored the idea, teamed me up with my talented coauthor Mark Johnston, and *Secret Agent* (Atheneum Books for Young Readers at Simon & Schuster, 2005) was born! Not only did Simon & Schuster scoop up the book, but they have already bought the sequel. Had I not taken a risk, been at the right place at the right time, I never would have met Ron and the book might still be living in my head."

interesting programs or hosting book signings? Are local colleges offering lecture series featuring writers, agents, and/or publishers?

Since many writers teach, investigate whether any well-known authors are teaching courses that you could attend in your area, even if it's just to sit in. Go where book people congregate and make contacts.

Specialties

Literary agents specialize in many kinds of books. Usually, their areas of interest are listed in the guidebooks and on their Web sites. You can also pick up books with topics that are similar to yours and look for the names of agents in the acknowledgment sections, where authors generally thank their agents. Frequently, it will say something like, "I wish to thank my agent _____ for her dedication throughout this entire book."

Even if you find an agent with the same specialty as your book, that agent might not be right for you—or you might not be right for him or her. How can you tell?

> *When an agent could be right for you:* When you approach the agent who just sold the hottest diet book with your time-tested diet book that is based on your long-running newspaper column called "Eating Right." It also doesn't hurt that you're a certified nutritionist who lectures frequently. Since the agent has experience with diet books plus the connections and knowledge of what diet books editors and publishers are buying, you just might have contacted the right agent.

> *Why that agent might not be right:* When you contact that agent about your diet book, the bar might be set so high that you don't have a chance. Since his or her recent success, that agent may have ascended to another level, representing only high-profile chefs and foodies with the most established national platforms. (A platform is the following and media presence that an author has built.)

Different Types of Agents

Some agents represent a variety of authors who write about many different fields. Some literary agencies have agents who specialize in different areas. If an agent or an agency doesn't handle your type of book, he or she usually can refer you to someone who does. And their recommendations can make a difference.

Start thinking of yourself in terms of your specialty areas. Are you a parenting writer, a memoir writer, a true-crime writer, a business writer, or a gardening writer? The more precisely you describe what you do, the more effectively you will be able to communicate with agents or people who can connect you with agents. Some of the most common categories (naturally, we can't include everything) are:

Fiction	Nonfiction	
Children's	Architecture	Humor
Fantasy	Art/Photography	Memoir
Foreign	Biography	Narrative
Martial arts	Business/Investment/Finance	Parenting
Middle grade	Celebrity	Pop science
Mystery/Crime	Cooking	Psychology
Romance	Design	Reference
Science fiction	Diet	Relationships
Thrillers	Entertaining	Self-help
Westerns	Food	Spirituality
Women's	Health/Fitness	Sports
Young adult	History/Politics/Current Affairs	Technology
	How-to	

Agents who specialize usually have terrific contacts with editors and publishers in their areas of interest. They are familiar with all of their books, the competition, their current lists, and their wish lists. Agents who specialize may draw upon a smaller but more focused pool of editors and publishers than agents who are generalists. The submission requirements will also differ for the type of book you plan to write. For example, cookbook editors will usually want to see some of the recipes you plan to include, photographs or illustrations of the finished food, and the text for the proposed book. Agents who specialize know the requirements and can tell you exactly what to submit.

Query Review

When agents receive a written submission from a potential client, their first thoughts are, "Is this a book that I want to handle and can I sell it?" Despite instructions on their Web sites and information in guidebooks, a large majority of the contacts agents receive are surprisingly not about books or subjects they handle.

Santa Monica agent Bonnie Solow, of Solow Literary Enterprises, says that she looks for "material that she feels extremely passionate about, that makes a positive contribution, is well written, marketable, and fresh." She also looks for writers with marketing platforms because those writers will "ignite a publisher's interest."

"For all authors, first time or established, what it all comes down to is having a marketable book idea," according to Jill Alexander, senior acquisitions editor at Adams Media. "This remains so even for authors who have published ten books. A marketable idea is something that fits with the house and is something that can be positioned and sold. The key is content, and do you have a good, marketable idea. It's very market-driven."

"Authors should focus narrowly," Alexander continues. "Is it saying something new to an established demographic, or, conversely, is it finding a new audience that is out there that hasn't been addressed that's actually pretty sizable? Many first-time authors mistakenly try to be everything to everyone. Instead, find out who your audience is—men or women, what age group, where do they work, what is their income level, what is their lifestyle, do they go to bookstores, how do they get their information, do they buy books or magazines, do they get their information from TV? Think about those questions," Alexander suggests.

The first thing agent Edward Knappman looks for is "a grabber in terms of the topic. Something that really grabs my attention in the first few lines or a topic that interests me personally. The grabber should excite me and be the same kind of hook that you would use in a proposal. Other important items that I look for are the writer's credentials, writing history, and platform. For business books, first-time writers need to have a platform," Knappman continues, "because the field is so competitive and it's hard to break out a business book when the author doesn't have a platform. Publishers want to know that they have some kind of following."

When New York City agent Peter Miller receives submissions, he asks:

1. Is the basic idea big enough, strong enough, or special enough to be published? Does it deserve to be a book?
2. Is there a structure: a beginning, middle, and end? Does it have a denouement, a climax? Is it enough for a whole meal or is it just a salad?
3. Did the writer simply tell readers the story or did the writer show or illustrate the story in ways that readers can see?

A writer who simply tells the story is a reporter, and repatorial writing is basically amateurish, Miller believes. A writer with true talent will show readers the story by reaching all the senses: can readers hear, smell, taste, and touch all of the words? Has the writer brought you into the room? Those elements create the writer's voice. "The main reason I reject submissions is because the writer doesn't have a voice," Miller explains. "Usually, writers have a good idea, a good plot, or the architecture of a book, but if there is no voice, I can't sell it."

When agents receive submissions from writers they're interested in, they send them their author/agent agreement, which they ask the writer to sign and return. Author/agent agreements will be discussed in detail in Chapter 13. Most agents try to get the author/agent agreement signed early in the relationship, before they perform a great deal of work.

Proposals

If a query piques an agent's interest, he or she will usually ask the writer to submit a written proposal. The agent may also contact the writer to ask questions and find out more about the project, or even ask for the entire manuscript, if it's already written.

Frequently, the requirements for proposal submissions are posted on agents' Web sites. Some have templates or provide their clients with examples that they want. Most just give general guidelines.

If the agent's site doesn't provide sufficient information, you can easily find what you need in a number of books, including our own *Author 101: Bestselling Book Proposals* (Adams Media, 2005).

Other helpful books on proposals are:

- *How to Write a Book Proposal,* by Michael Larsen (Writer's Digest Books, 2004).
- *The Art of the Book Proposal: From Focused Idea to Finished Proposal,* by Eric Maisel, Ph.D. (Jeremy P. Tarcher/Penguin, 2004).

Agents tell us that they seldom receive proposals that don't need help. But agents differ sharply regarding the help they provide.

Some agents are editorially intensive; they do hands-on editing and work closely with writers to reshape their proposals until they get them just right. These agents believe that the quality of the proposal reflects upon them, so they work hard to submit only the best proposals to publishers.

Other agents will make minor edits to a proposal or suggest structural changes that writers should make. However, they won't do extensive editing or rewriting. If a proposal requires more than minor work, the most they will do is tell the writer what it needs.

Frequently, writers can't make the necessary changes. Even the best writers need editors because it's so difficult for them to objectively analyze their own work. So they need professional writers or editors to fix their proposals. In these situations, some agents will give writers names or recommendations to writing professionals, while others will not.

"It's hard for agents to write back and tell writers how they could make their books better and more salable," Roger Cooper, executive vice-president of I Books, Incorporated, reveals. "Some agents may be editorially intensive, but many have now become the same type of traffic managers that editors have become. They traffic products instead of working on them, adding creative input and massaging, tickling, and teasing them until they get to a certain standard. Now, many agents are essentially screeners for publishers."

In fact, many agents will not edit, rewrite, critique, or even tell writers why they rejected their proposals. A number of the agents we interviewed had editorial and publishing backgrounds and regretted that the demands on their time made it impossible for them to be more editorially involved.

San Francisco agent Michael Larsen of the Larsen-Pomada Literary Agency does hands-on editing to refine his clients' proposals. When we spoke with him about an agent's input on proposals, here's what he told us: "This goes to the heart of what agents can do for writers and what writers can't do for themselves—make sure that the proposal is as good as it can be before it's sent out. This means being aware of what editors expect to find in proposals. Writers usually don't know this because they haven't dealt with editors."

"Editors expect every word to be right, and the proposal to be as enjoyable as possible to read," Larsen continues. "The objective is to give them as many reasons as possible to say yes to the proposal and not a single reason to say no. The reasons why an editor will say yes include: The book idea is compelling, the writer writes well and has a platform, is promotable, and has a strong promotion plan. Also that the book has great style, potential as a series, subsidiary rights potential, and good timing."

Matchmaking

After the proposal has been edited and is ready for submission, agents begin what many consider the most important part of their work: coming up with a list of editors who could be interested in buying the book. Matching editors and publishing houses with projects is an art. Many considerations must be factored in, such as:

- What kinds of books is a house buying?
- What have they bought in the past or do they want in the future?
- What's on their list and what gaps do they have to fill?
- In what directions are they moving and what are their platform demands?

"When I get something that piques my interest, I think: What editors do I know that would feel as excited as I do about this project?" agent June Clark relates. "If a half dozen or so people come to mind, then I feel secure that it's a project I want to take on, because the job of an agent is to know who's buying what at publishing houses—it's being a matchmaker. You have to know the tastes of editors, because when you find those type of works, you're eager to represent the authors because it increases your confidence level."

Most agents keep detailed records on everyone they've worked with in publishing. Some build databases that contain editors' and publishers' names, contact information, what they've bought and worked on, as well as their likes, dislikes, and publishing history. Other agents simply rely on their memories, knowledge, and experiences with editors and the industry.

"We know and have established relationships with editors and know what they're buying," agent Edward Knappman says. "We maintain a fairly sophisticated database of editors and their interests, on which we record about 150 categories of books they buy. Every time an editor is listed in *Publishers Lunch* as having bought something, we add that information to our database. So we have a profile on virtually every editor at the significant publishing houses and what they bought in the past and what they're now buying. We have also built many close relationships with agents."

Keeping abreast of who's where and what they're buying can be a challenge because the publishing world is constantly in transition. "It changes so frequently," June Clark explains. "There are times when you have a great rapport with an editor and she leaves. They may take jobs with another publishing house, not buy the same type of books, leave publishing entirely, or become agents. But some publishing companies are very stable. They have a core group of editors who have been there for years."

Agents keep current by regularly reading industry publications like *Publishers Lunch*, *Publishers Weekly*, and some of the many blogs that are now written on writing and publishing. *Publishers Lunch* reports recent book sales and states which editors and houses bought each book. Agents also attend conferences and events with other agents, editors, and publishing professionals.

"It's a people business where relationships rule. Most agents really like people; they're friendly and outgoing and enjoy socializing. Being an agent is about making friends; it's about spending time with people who have similar tastes, likes, and dislikes. People in publishing tend to think of the industry as a family, so they'll usually be happy to help and extend themselves for family members."

Agents keep in contact by frequently meeting with editors and publishing people, usually over lunch. When they meet, the agents will ask what the editors and publishers are working on, what they're interested in, and what they need.

Agents headquartered in and around New York City often make it a practice to meet editors and other agents for lunch. Some belong to agent lunch groups that get together every month. These groups have about ten members, and four to eight usually show up at each of the lunches. They have no agenda, but common interests are discussed. Every once in a while, someone will say, "I have a problem," and they will discuss it.

Meeting with editors and other agents is also a necessary part of the business for out-of-town agents. For example, San Francisco agents Mike Larsen and his partner, Elizabeth Pomada, travel to New York City twice a year, in the spring and fall, to renew acquaintances and meet editors. On each visit, they see between 75 and 100 editors.

June Clark tells us that when she sees or hears something about an editor whom she doesn't know, she will call to find out about him or her, what he or she is interested in and what's on his or her list. Usually, editors are enthusiastic because they're always looking for good material.

"Editors also contact me and say that they don't know me, but they read that I just sold this book, which they would have been interested in," Clark states. "Then they will ask me what I have going. Basically, they make contact to see if there's some synergy there and to build a relationship."

Agents also keep in contact with other agents by attending industry events. In New York, AAR, the agents' association, hosts monthly programs, including one called Meet the Publisher. At these events, representatives from publishing companies bring some of their editors to tell the group about developments at their houses. AAR also puts on programs on subjects of interest to agents, such as copyright, contracts, and recent industry developments.

Working Together with Your Agent

Don't be afraid to ask agents for the names of the publishers to whom they will be submitting your books. Many agents are also open to suggestions from authors regarding which publishers to approach. However, trust their judgment; remember they are skilled professionals and they often excel at matching books with buyers.

The key is not to bother agents with calls. Let them do their job. Don't constantly ask, "Have you heard from so and so?" Instead, maintain your own records and when you receive rejections, check them off your list. While keeping such records is obviously a part of your agent's job, keeping your own records will keep you informed so you won't have to needlessly bother your agent. Occasionally, schedule a time to call your agent to review the progress on your proposal. But give your agent sufficient time to succeed, and don't repeatedly call.

Submissions

When agents come up with a list of editors, they make multiple submissions of the proposal. They may submit it to ten or more editors, depending on the nature of the book. Agents will sometimes send proposals to two or more imprints that are owned by the same parent company. However, some companies such as Doubleday and Broadway Books, which are imprints owned by Random House, both have the same editorial board. So an agent would not submit the same proposal to editors at both of those imprints.

Unlike writers, agents have this special knowledge, which can save them substantial time, energy, expense, and embarrassment.

Before agents send proposals to editors, they usually send them the equivalent of a query letter asking if they might be interested in the book. Queries are sent only when the proposal is ready. Queries can be sent via e-mail or hard copy, depending on the nature of the book and the editor's preference.

If an editor asks to see a proposal, it can be sent by e-mail, hard copy, or both. Editors expect that other editors will have received the proposal, and will usually move more quickly on those that elicit their interest. To entice editors and generate more interest in a proposal, agents will tell editors when other editors are interested in a property.

When a proposal includes items such as a self-published edition of the book, illustrations or artwork, they must be submitted in hard copy. Hard-copy submissions are accompanied by a short cover letter that itemizes all materials sent. Sometimes, agents will set time limits in which editors must make offers.

When proposals are submitted by e-mail, the cover letter includes a link to the proposal that editors can download. They can also request a hard copy that can be forwarded under separate cover.

Sharlene Martin, of Martin Literary Management in Encino, California, submits proposals either electronically, as PDF files, or in hard copy, depending on what the editor requests. Electronic submissions allow editors to transmit proposals to their colleagues without having to photocopy them. "If you have several editors interested, sending a proposal electronically can move it more quickly so they can make an immediate offer," Martin notes.

Robyn Says

"When my nonfiction agent submits a book proposal, I let her take the lead and decide when to inform me how it's going. I would drive her crazy, and me as well, if I called every other day asking about the status of each submission. It's important to let agents do their job.

"Over the years we've made an unspoken agreement. She sends me rejections via fax or mail, but when great news arrives, she calls me. If I'm not in, she puts out an APB for me. Then, my office, husband, and family members make it a mission to find me! They all know that her calls are top priority!"

Author 101 ■ Bestselling Secrets from Top Agents

38

When Martin sends hard-copy proposals, she always prints and attaches the e-mails that she and editors have exchanged. With a bright, bold marker, she highlights the editor's language requesting the proposal. "This reminds them that it's not being sent to them cold, that they requested it," Martin explains.

Martin doesn't include a cover letter with the package, but usually attaches her business card and writes, "Thanks _____ (the editor's name). Enjoy the read!" She tries not to bog them down with more paper.

Editors are increasingly receptive of receiving proposals electronically. The two main considerations in sending proposals are making sure to include (1) what the editor has to see and (2) what the editor wants to see.

Editors are swamped, and it's a challenge for them to read everything they receive. If they're interested, they usually get back to the agent quickly, within a week or two.

Many editors have their assistants screen submissions, so if their assistants like a proposal, it may speed up their response time. If editors don't get back to an agent within a week or two, it usually means that the book is not going to sell.

When Editors Are Interested

When an editor expresses interest in a proposal, agents inform the other editors to whom they submitted the proposal. This provides an incentive for them to get to the project. Interested editors present the proposal to their editorial boards or those who have the authority to buy the book.

Editorial boards usually meet weekly. Houses have differing schedules, which good agents should know in order to set deadlines and figure when they should expect responses.

When several houses are interested in a property, auctions can be held. However, auctions are not common. In an auction, agents give editors the date when bids must be submitted. After the first round of bids, they inform all the participants of the amount of the highest bids and continue requesting bids until one house wins. Another auction technique is to request a single, best bid. In these auctions, all bidders must submit their best and only offer by a set date and time.

When they try to sell books, agents usually approach larger publishing houses first because they pay more. If they can't sell a book to a big house, agents focus their attention on selling it to smaller firms. For some authors, it can be better to have a big book at a smaller house than to have a small book at a big house where it can get lost.

Whenever possible, authors should try to arrange a face-to-face meeting with editors who are thinking about buying their books. These meetings can give editors an incentive to read the writer's proposal, especially if the writer is making a special trip to town.

Tête-à-têtes with authors can also show editors that an author is personable, well spoken, and promotable. These visits can be valuable to iron out problems; to reshape the book's organization, direction, or format; and to help cement a solid working rapport.

Negotiation

When a publisher makes an initial offer, negotiations begin. Agents are usually experienced and savvy negotiators. They usually know the current market, the price similar books have brought, and what the house will pay. Since their income is contingent on the amounts their clients receive, agents can usually be relied on to work diligently for the best possible deal.

Agents also understand publishing contracts. They know which clauses are boilerplate and cannot be changed and which can be changed and to what degree. As seasoned negotiators, agents usually have developed an instinct for when they should give, when they should stand firm, and how hard they should push.

Conflicts of interest can arise if agents have other deals pending or long-standing relationships with a publisher. In these cases, trade-offs and compromises are not unheard of, and the interests of one client may be compromised for the benefit of another client or of the agent.

When all parties agree on the contract terms, the publisher drafts and submits a contract to the agent for review. Before sending out contracts, some publishers send out memorandums of agreement or understanding that clarify the terms that were agreed on. Memos may also be sent when the terms are complex or unusual. Occasionally, subsequent negotiations may be required to clarify misunderstandings or issues that were not fully addressed.

When full agreement is reached, agents have their clients sign the contract. They then submit the executed contracts to the publisher and wait for the first advance payment, which is usually payable on the signing of the contract. When the advance money comes in, they deposit the check in a trust account, take their cut, and disburse the client's share by check.

Postcontract

After the contract is signed, the author completes the book. During this time, problems may arise. Authors and editors often clash or disagree over items, including content, structure, language, and writing style. Other issues may arise concerning cover design, distribution, and promotion.

Agents often get involved to act as their clients' advocate. They may act as mediators or go-betweens in disputes and try to reach compromises to resolve them. Frequently, agents will have to reason with, educate, or settle down unrealistic or paranoid clients; set them straight; and explain the facts of publishing life.

An agent's most significant role may be as a writer's confidant. When a book is being written, an agent may be the only person an author can speak to or confide in regarding the project. The agent may be the only other soul who really understands the project, the problems or decisions facing the writer, and the ramifications of the choices the writer may be required to make. In these situations, agents serve as writers' advisors, teachers, mentors, and friends.

Some clients can become extremely needy and insecure. So their agents assume the roles of therapists and best friends. Agent/author relationships can be close and intense. New York City agent Peter Miller has such a close relationship with a client that the client calls Miller his "second wife."

After a book has been written, agents supervise and make sure that the publisher is living up to its contractual commitments. Agents will track book sales and scrutinize royalty statements and information they receive from publishers. They will also check on the sales of subsidiary rights such as audiobooks, foreign rights, products, and motion picture rights.

If a book is doing well, an agent will usually push publishers for more benefits. These can include providing more focused promotion, printing additional copies of the book, or signing the author for subsequent books.

Your Next Book

After a book has been written, agent Bonnie Solow feels that authors and their agents should not simply be reactive to what the next book will be. "Instead, they should come up with a plan to architect a publishing career that embodies the trends that people are interested in and sparks the client's interest and commitment," Solow advises. So she does a lot of editorial career management by brainstorming and designing a long-term plan.

Solow also helps her clients market their books by recommending outside publicists and media coaches. She has also helped them land infomercials, launch Web sites, and arrange speaking engagements and merchandising agreements, and has consulted with them on film deals and TV series. "I get excited about a project when I feel that the writer's content and personality will work beyond the bookstore shelf," she reports.

Action Steps

1. How do most agents want to be initially contacted?
2. Name five types of books in which an agent might specialize.
3. When agents respond positively to writers' initial queries, what do they usually ask the writers to submit?
4. How do agents stay current and up on industry developments?
5. Do agents simultaneously send submissions to more than one publishing house?

Remember:

 Most agents want writers to contact them initially via e-mail. They want written submissions so they can get a sense of the writers' ability to express themselves, and to see how well writers are organized and their skill in presenting themselves and their ideas. If they are intrigued, they will ask the writer to send them a book proposal. Frequently, agents' submission requirements are posted on their Web sites.

 Agents vary as to how much editing or revising of proposals they will do. Some are editorially intensive while others will make only minor edits. When agents find a proposal acceptable, they will create a list of editors who they think might be interested in the book. Then, they will contact those editors and send the proposals to those who express interest. If an editor is interested in buying the property, the agent will negotiate the terms of sale and review the contract.

CHAPTER	"A writer is a person for whom writing is more difficult than it is
4	for other people."
	Thomas Mann

So Why an Agent?

THIS CHAPTER WILL COVER:

▶ Agents as salespersons
▶ The advantages of agents

AT SOME POINT in their careers, most writers come face-to-face with the question of whether they should hire a literary agent. Usually, they know that an agent can increase the odds of getting their book published, but securing one can be an ordeal. Plus, an agent will be entitled to a chunk of whatever their writings earn.

To help you make your decision, we have compiled a list of the advantages of agents. However, before we get into those advantages, we would like to share some of the lessons we have learned over the years.

Literary agents come in all sizes, shapes, and competencies. They range from being highly conscientious, extremely professional, and totally trustworthy to being disagreeable, incompetent, or just plain crooked. That said, most agents do a very good job and represent their clients well. However, as in any other business, sharks and barracudas occasionally troll the waters. Make sure that you know whom you're dealing with before you sign on.

If you hire an agent, that person will be your partner, so it's essential to know what an agent should provide. You should first understand that a major part of an agent's job is to function essentially as a salesperson, which is not a negative factor. Some facts about agents:

- Agents are highly connected salespeople.
- Agents are some of the best matchmakers that ever walked the earth.
- Many agents are remarkably intuitive; they seem to have heightened perceptions and great gut feelings about authors and their books.
- Agents know writing. They can often see those special sparks that others generally miss; many are visionaries who can predict what will sell.

Call them talent scouts, call them literary agents—many of them are extraordinary individuals who excel at bringing great ideas to life.

The business of agents is to find properties to sell to publishers. Since they work on a percentage of the amounts their clients receive, they usually try to obtain the best possible terms for their clients. In some cases, this may be a big advance, a lucrative royalty structure, and a strong commitment to a publicity campaign. In certain situations, they may accept less money to place their client with a particular publishing house or to get more promotion.

Agents' business revolves around their interpersonal relationships. They can be delightful and charming and sweep starry-eyed clients off their feet. After all, it's flattering to be represented by a literary agent and to be in the company of celebrated writers in the agent's stable, especially if it's a well-known and highly regarded agent.

Despite the attention agents may lavish on you, never forget that writers are commodities to agents; clients and the work they produce are agents' stock-in-trade. Regardless of how close you and your agent become and how much you like him or her, never lose sight of the fact that you are involved in a business relationship.

Advantages of Agents

Agents can provide invaluable help to writers. The following are some of the things that an agent can offer a writer.

Advantage #1: Clout

Proposals and manuscripts that are submitted by agents have a much greater chance of being published than those sent directly by writers. Publishers assume that agents have screened submissions and that they are of a higher caliber than those submitted directly by writers. Editors tend to rely on agents who, in dealings with them, have consistently demonstrated that they will submit only work that meets high standards.

Advantage #2: Knowledge of Books

Most agents can tell if your project has merit and if you have the talent and ability to write a salable manuscript. A professional literary representative can see the potential in raw, insufficiently developed

Rick Says

"Without an agent it's increasingly difficult to get your proposal or manuscript read by a publisher. More and more, publishing houses are refusing to accept unsolicited and unagented manuscripts. Those that do, usually assign them to their slush piles to be read by less experienced, junior editors who are highly overworked and frequently exhausted and irritable. Few manuscripts from the slush piles get published.

"Some editors will read proposals submitted by agents for books by writers who do not have national platforms. However, the editors must have great respect for those agents. And even if they like those projects, they may not be able to sell them to their houses."

submissions and suggest changes to your proposal or manuscript that will make it more attractive to publishers and, ultimately, the public. For example, he or she may suggest format changes to your proposal's promotion plan that you would have never considered.

Agents know what editors and publishers want and how to tailor proposals and manuscripts for them. They also know how, when, and to whom to make submissions as well as what to avoid or downplay. Agents are also great estimators and have a feel for what a book is worth.

Advantage #3: Resources

Good agents can spot defects in submissions that are fixable. They can identify holes in your facts, logic, approach, or writing style that would doom your project and cause publishers to reject it. If your manuscript or proposal has merit but needs work to sell, an agent can recommend the right people to help you fix it.

Many agents are reluctant to recommend particular resource people and others will prefer to give you the names of several from which you can choose. They usually know and have had experience with people who can help writers at every stage, including editors, indexers, fact checkers, ghostwriters, and media trainers.

Advantage #4: Understanding of the Market

Good agents know what's selling and what's not. They make it their business to find out which houses and editors are buying, what type of manuscripts they are accepting and rejecting and precisely what they are looking for. Agents know what similar properties have sold for and which houses will pay the top price.

Agents also closely follow the publishing business. They know the market, the deals recently made and the prices they commanded. They also know what's in the pipeline and the industry buzz. To keep up to date on the trends, agents read everything available on which house sold what and what's going on in the industry. They know the topics that are oversaturated, the subject areas that are in demand and the books that are flying out of the stores.

Agents have a wide array of publishing contacts, including those with whom they have worked successfully in the past. And they make it a point to stay in touch with their contacts. Agents understand the industry hierarchy and know the best order in which to make submissions to various publishing houses.

Advantage #5: Timing

Working through an agent can also get your book read and published quicker. Your proposal or manuscript will usually be read well before those that are tossed on the slush pile. When an agent represents you, negotiating and processing contracts usually takes less time.

Since good agents understand the publishing industry and the market, they know the best time to make submissions and when to hold them back. And, as we're sure you know, timing can be everything. In addition to understanding the overall market, agents keep abreast of the conditions at many publishing houses.

Advantage #6: Contacts

Most agents have worked in publishing and have extensive industry contacts. They know what editors want, need, like, and dislike. Often, agents will have worked directly with the very editors and publishers that they are pitching. When these agents make representations or commitments, editors and publishers know that they can rely on them.

Advantage #7: Negotiating Skills

Agents are usually terrific negotiators. Since they get a piece of the action, they have a strong financial incentive to negotiate the best possible deals. Ideally, they will try to conduct an auction in which several publishers bid against one another to buy your book.

Agents understand publishing contracts. They know which clauses to include and exclude, the royalty percentages obtainable and the best ways to get them. They also know the amounts to demand for subsidiary rights and what to request with regard to other rights, including

Robyn Says

"Literary agents know where to find editors and are brilliant at making matches. Their connections can be the key in helping you get a book deal. In publishing, people constantly change jobs and companies. So good agents make it a point to know where they relocated to and how to reach them.

"In the case of my book *The GIFTionary* (St. Martin's Griffin, 2003), my agent introduced me to Jennifer Enderlin, an editor who really inspired me. We hit it off and she showed a sincere interest in my ideas, which resulted in the initial book as well as a follow-up titled *Make It Memorable* (2004).

"Smart and dedicated agents work like crazy to stay in contact with their contacts; they speak regularly, go to lunch, and meet at industry-related events. They also seek out and reach out to editors they don't know to find out about their lists and their needs. Their passion for your book fuels the effort, so it's key that you team up with an agent who really believes in your writing, talents, and abilities."

options, escalator clauses, and promotion. If something gets very sticky, they know the right lawyers to call.

Advantage #8: Career Management

Agents understand that publishers prefer to work with authors who will write multiple books. Therefore, they can position you for future projects not only during contract negotiations, but also after the deal has been sealed. For example, if your first book gets strong reviews or sells well, agents can immediately push for more promotion, including national tours, serialization, and the placement of excerpts and quotes. They can also jump-start negotiations for subsequent books.

Advantage #9: Strong Representation

Good agents will make sure that publishers are fulfilling their contractual obligations. Conflicts always arise between authors and their editors and publishers; it's inherent in the business. When they do, your agent should act as your representative to fight for your interest.

Publishers have been known to be sloppy with their bookkeeping, accounting, and reporting practices, and to make mistakes. Agents, as part of their duty in representing you, should scrutinize statements and accounts and make sure everything is in order.

Advantage #10: Increased Income

Agents often make more money for you. Great agents more than earn their 15 percent and frequently can get you more money as well. They know what a project is worth, what it will bring in and the houses that are paying top dollar. They know when to push for a larger advance or more desirable terms.

Agents can spot additional profit centers for a book and often have the connections to link you up. Since they know the market and the industry, they know what subsidiary rights can be sold and how much they should return. They can also get you beneficial contract clauses such as those specifying bonuses if your book meets certain goals.

They are not afraid to ask publishers to pay what a book deserves. Often, first-time authors are so eager to get their books published that they will jump on inadequate offers. Most authors feel that their agents earn more for them than they cost. Agents are knowledgeable industry experts and their business is to make both of you money.

Advantage #11: Advice

Writing can be an isolated occupation: Many writers work alone and are forced to figure out endless problems on their own. Frequently, they have no one to discuss their problems with and no one to just talk with about their writing and its nuances. Agents can fill that gap.

Most agents were writers, editors, or otherwise involved in publishing before they became writers' representatives. So they generally understand the writing process. When writers are working on projects, their agents may be the only people with whom they can commiserate about a project or a problem with that project. An agent may be the only person the writer can bounce ideas off of and the only one who fully understands the difficulties or subtleties involved.

During writing projects, writers may need to talk about their projects, vent their anger or frustration, or share their joys or disappointments. Frequently, agents have been through similar situations and they can tell writers how to proceed. Sometimes, the mere fact that agents are there for writers, that they lend a sympathetic or supportive ear, is all writers need.

Advantage #12: Prestige

Being represented by a respected or well-known agent can give a writer greater standing in his or her community and in publishing circles. For example, if an agent is noted for handling the top business writers, signing with that agent can give authors additional status in the business world. Acceptance by a respected agent could indicate that the author has reached a certain plateau in his or her specialty field(s).

An agent's reputation could also be helpful with publishers, especially those houses that specialize in the area that the agent handles. Publishers often cultivate close relationships with such agents because they can ensure a flow of top talent to the house.

Action Steps

1. List three reasons why agents may have clout with publishers.
2. Give five examples of agents' knowledge that can help writers.
3. Explain how an agent's understanding of the market can help writers.
4. In what ways can agents police publishers on behalf of their clients?
5. Explain how agents can get their clients more money.

Remember:

 If you hire an agent, he or she will be your partner. A major part of an agent's job is to be a salesperson, to sell your book and the rights it may generate. Material submitted to publishers by agents has a greater chance of being published than work sent directly by writers. Agents know good, salable writing and what publishers want. They also know how to improve or fix writing problems.

 Agents are professional negotiators and experts on publishing contracts. They can usually get you more than you would receive if you represented yourself. Literary agents can be indispensable career builders, advisors, and managers. And being represented by an agent can give you added prestige.

CHAPTER 5

"How vain is it to sit down to write when you have not stood up to live?"

Henry David Thoreau

So Why Not an Agent?

THIS CHAPTER WILL COVER:

▶ Agents as salespeople
▶ The disadvantages of agents

NOW THAT YOU KNOW the advantages of literary agents, let's look at the other side—the disadvantages. The fact that literary agents are such accomplished salespeople can be a double-edged sword. On the plus side, their compensation is based on what their clients earn. So agents try to get their writers top dollar.

On the minus side, literary agents often face conflicts because the interests of their clients may differ from those of publishers with whom they work. During these conflicts, they may decide that it is more important to further a publisher's interests than to further those of their client. When this occurs, the same traits that make agents such marvelous salespeople can be turned on their clients to sell them real estate in Outer Mongolia. Agents are typically charming and engaging and wrap themselves in cloaks of trust, but when their interests are at stake, some of the weaker members of the guild protect what they see as their long-term interests and not their clients.

Disadvantages of Agents

In most situations, agents do accelerate the publishing process for writers. However, many highly successful authors have elected not to employ agents to represent them. They prefer to personally have direct contact with their publishers and eliminate the middleman or -woman.

These exceptions to the rule believe that they are their own best representatives. They are confident that they can do a better job than agents can in protecting their own interests. And, they know that if they need help, they can always hire the top literary or publishing attorneys and other outstanding professionals.

Some of the reasons that might influence writers not to hire literary agents are listed below.

Disadvantage #1: Expense

In most cases, first-time authors don't make money on their books. If you factor in all the time they spend researching, writing, and trying to get their books published, they usually come out in the red. When you add agents' fees to the mix, writers' losses increase.

Many writers think they can't afford to hire an agent or that it doesn't make financial sense. However, the opposite may be true, especially in terms of long-term career decisions.

With an agent, writers can make more money. If an agent will take a writer on, it means that at least one professional believes that the writer shows promise, so others might react similarly. An agent can help writers develop that promise and move them and their careers in the right direction, which may be impossible for writers to do on their own.

Disadvantage #2: A "Sales First" Attitude

Since agents are commissioned salespersons, they may be more protective of their financial interests than your writing career. Under most agency contracts, you cannot use another agent, except for writing that is in an area they do not specialize in. However, agents can serve other clients and conflicts can arise.

Robyn Says

"The key to the agent/author relationship is securing an agent who doesn't just want a quick sale (even though a quick sale is an author's dream, and we definitely aren't knocking that). You want an agent who really sees promise in your work and is dedicated to helping you build your career.

"To hook up with that kind of agent, you have to show up with the goods. However, even the most accomplished authors need someone to bounce ideas off of and come to for honest feedback. A meaningful agent/author relationship can result in new book ideas and exciting opportunities and can result in creating valuable literary contributions. Be smart, figure out what you want in an agent and fully check him or her out before you sign on. Try to find one who will help you build your career and stick with you for the long haul."

To make a sale, agents could move your book in a direction in which you don't want to move. Although their judgments could make your book more salable, it may not be how you want to shape your career.

Disadvantage #3: Dual Loyalty

Since agents rely heavily on their industry connections and they represent other writers, their duties to you could be compromised. Conflicts of interest come with a literary agent's territory. Some agents handle potential conflicts with a high degree of integrity, but others may not always be able to resist the temptation because of their own self-interests.

Weaker agents may trade off or sacrifice what's best for you to maintain a good industry contact or to help another client. They may weigh a decision on the basis of how it could impact their career as opposed to its effect on your book, which just might be a one-shot deal for them.

Agents can also spread themselves too thin and not give all of their clients adequate attention. Agents must balance what's best for their clients, their publishing industry contacts, and themselves, which is often tricky.

Disadvantage #4: Questions of Competence

No licensing requirements or competency standards exist for literary agents. Anyone can call himself or herself an agent. So, the variation between agents and the level of representation you receive can be enormous. Unfortunately, many writers won't know or be able to tell the difference until it's too late. The best protection is to thoroughly research prospective agents and get recommendations from their present and past clients.

Incompetent individuals have entered the field because the demand for agents is so great, and this has caused significant damage. Some incompetent agents may try hard and mean well, but they don't have the necessary knowledge or ability to offer the level of protection and representation that writers deserve. Do your research before you agree to let an agent represent you or give him or her any payment.

Disadvantage #5: Time

Finding the right agent takes valuable time. Since getting an agent can be hard, many writers go with the first one who shows interest in them. In doing so, they often get involved with an agent who is a poor fit for them. Before you contact any agents, conduct research. Learn about the industry and what agents provide. Read the guidebooks to get an understanding of the composition of each agency, its areas of interest, its successes, and its overall approach. Check agents' Web sites.

Some authors would rather spend their time writing or with their families and friends rather than trying to get an agent. It can be frustrating and even humiliating when no agents seem interested or none call back or think that your book has merit. In these situations, writers don't bother or they simply move on.

Disadvantage #6: A Lack of Guarantees

The fact that an agent represents you doesn't guarantee that your book will sell. It doesn't even guarantee that your agent will work diligently to get your book published. In addition, agents may pile up expenses in trying to peddle your book that they may bill you for even though your book didn't sell.

Agents can also encourage you to change or revise your work, which can cost you time and money and still not guarantee a sale.

Disadvantage #7: Occasional Crooks

Again, the absence of licensing or certification requirements for literary agents plus the lack of enforceable standards of conduct has made the business vulnerable to the dishonest. As in any other business, some unscrupulous people do become agents. Although they are in the vast minority, unfortunately, some do exist. Some of their shady practices include charging their clients fees for reading and submitting their materials and charging handling fees and excessive, marked-up expenses. They may also give and take kickbacks, may not submit their clients' work to publishers as promised, or may simply pocket their clients' royalties.

Crooked agents may also refer their clients to services that provide a kickback to them or that they have a financial interest in. These can include editors, designers, Web designers, illustrators, publicists, and vanity publishers. Research all potential agents before you do business with them and don't pay them a dime; any payments they receive should come from royalties you earn.

Disadvantage #8: Possibly Better Alternatives

In certain situations, it may be better to be represented by a lawyer than an agent. For example, if your book is an extension of your business, a book deal may affect your interests in ways a literary agent is not capable of handling. Or you could be an academic who needs to be published but doesn't want to build a writing career. In many major U.S. cities, you can hire lawyers who are expert at handling publishing contracts. Often, the cost of hiring even the most expensive attorney can be much cheaper than paying an agent at least 15 percent of the income you receive.

Disadvantage #9: Too Much Trouble

Many writers cannot get agents to represent them. Others find the courting process hard, frustrating, and enervating—it saps their strength. They feel that the time, effort, and aggravation may just not be worth it. The experience of trying to find an agent can be disheartening and discouraging and many writers give up. It leaves them somewhat wounded. Fighting discouragement is a constant battle for many writers. It's hard to keep your spirits up when everyone is rejecting you and your work. So, many writers, to maintain their mental health, decide to go it alone, without a literary agent, and spare themselves further painful disillusionment.

Disadvantage #10: Great Editorial Contacts of Your Own

If you have great editorial contacts, long-standing relationships with editors and publishers, and a good understanding of publishing, an agent may be unnecessary. It may be more desirable for you to hire an attorney who specializes in publishing law to negotiate and/or review your contract.

However experienced you may be, don't delude yourself into thinking that you have more publishing smarts than you actually might

"Publishing is a specialized business and unless you are also an industry insider, having editorial contacts may just not be enough. Without an agent, you may be out of your depth. For a few dollars saved in fees, don't chance entering into a deal that you may regret. Even if you don't want to hire an agent, consider having a literary and publishing law attorney first check anything you're asked to sign."

have. Also, don't think that your publishing contacts will place your interests above theirs. To make sure that someone is on your side, get professional help from either an agent or a lawyer.

Action Steps

1. Explain how agents' talents as salespersons can hurt their clients.
2. Describe the inherent conflict of interest that agents face.
3. Does hiring an agent guarantee that your book will be published?
4. What are the licensing requirements and competency standards for literary agents?
5. What alternatives to literary agents do writers have?

Remember:

 Agents generally make more for authors than those authors would receive representing themselves. This is usually the case, even though paying agents' commissions can be costly. However, being an agent involves inherent conflicts of interest, and some agents may be more interested in protecting their financial interests than in carrying out their duties to their clients.

 Since no licensing requirements or competency standards exist for agents, anyone can call himself or herself an agent. Therefore, the variation in the level of representation clients receive can be huge, and some agents are just plain dishonest. The fact that authors hire agents does not guarantee that their books will sell, and getting an agent can be difficult and time-consuming.

CHAPTER 6

"You never get a second chance to make a good first impression."
Will Rogers

Before You Contact an Agent

THIS CHAPTER WILL COVER:

▶ Educate yourself
▶ Research agents
▶ Keep records
▶ Build a platform
▶ Be ready
▶ Your opening pitch
▶ Expectations

WHEN WRITERS BEGIN their search for an agent, they're often lax. They don't properly prepare. In most cases, they don't start with a solid plan of attack and follow it systematically. So, if and when an agent expresses interest, they're not in a position to make the most of that golden opportunity.

Lack of preparation can lead to a string of disheartening rejections. Then, if they're lucky enough to get a subsequent nibble from another agent, they tend to leap on board and frequently make poor matches.

Most writers don't understand what it takes to interest an agent. Usually, they are so consumed by their writing that they don't think about anything else. They convince themselves that if they write a great book, it will find its market—and the right agent. Sadly, that's not always the case. Finding the right agent takes time, work, and effort. Save yourself pain, expense, and disillusionment by developing a detailed plan before you start your agent hunt, and then follow it. Make it a separate project distinct from the writing of your book. Give it your full attention and focus your efforts on gathering sufficient information to find the best agent for you.

Don't contact an agent unless you:

1. Know exactly whom you're dealing with. Check the agency's Web site and the guidebooks to learn what types of books the agency handles, its submission requirements, and the authors it represents. We will tell you how to proceed in this chapter.
2. Know precisely what you're going to say. We will cover this in the section called "Your Opening Pitch."
3. Have submissions ready in the event the agent requests them. An agent could ask for a query letter, a book proposal, your entire manuscript, or other submissions. Visit the agency's Web site and look it up in the guidebooks to learn what may be required.

Educate Yourself

The first step in your mission to obtain an agent is to educate yourself about the literary agency business. Learn everything you can—how the business works, what agents do, how they do it, and what you should expect of them.

Start generally by developing an overall understanding of the literary agency business. Then, zero in on specific agents or agencies that deal with books like yours and that interest you. Read books on the topic; several are listed below. They each cover the subject somewhat differently, so read as many as you can to gain an understanding of the agency business and agents. Books that can provide a good overview include:

■ *Literary Agents: What They Do, How They Do It, and How to Find and Work with the Right One for You*, by Michael Larsen (John Wiley & Sons, 1996).

- *Agents, Editors and You: The Insider's Guide to Getting Your Book Published,* by Michelle Howry (Writer's Digest Books, 2002).
- *How to Be Your Own Literary Agent: An Insider's Guide to Getting Your Book Published,* by Richard Curtis (Houghton Mifflin, 2003).
- *Be Your Own Literary Agent: The Ultimate Insider's Guide to Getting Published,* by Martin P. Levin (Ten Speed Press, 1996).
- *Literary Agents: A Writer's Introduction,* by John F. Baker (Macmillan, 1999).

To see what publishers are buying, subscribe to *Publishers Lunch* (*www.publishersmarketplace.com/lunch/free/*) and other online newsletters. *Publishers Lunch,* which is free, provides industry news and lists recent book sales. It names the agents, authors, and publishers involved and categorizes sales by:

- "Nice deals"—$1 to $100,000
- "Good deals"—$101,000 to $250,000
- "Significant deals"—$251,000 to $500,000
- "Major deals"—$501,000 and up

When you spot the names of agents who have just sold a similar or simpatico book to your own, do your research and then contact them.

You should also read *Writer's Digest* magazine. It's aimed at writers, and it often includes pieces that can give you information about agents and the literary agency business. It also gives you a good perspective about the industry and what subjects are of current interest. And don't forget to read articles on the Internet, which is now teeming with blogs and good information.

When you acquire a general understanding of the agency business, focus on spotting which individual agents or agencies could be right for you. A number of guidebooks and online guides set forth agents' contact information, areas of specialty and interest, as well as information on their businesses. Some also contain helpful articles on agents and other aspects of publishing. The guidebooks include:

Guide to Book Publishers, Editors, & Literary Agents, by Jeff Herman (The Writer Books, published annually). This is the most comprehensive of the guidebooks. It gives extensive background information on agents, their areas of interest, and areas in which they have no interest. It breaks down information provided for the individual agents in the firm, and it lists the best way to contact each, their client representation by category, commission charged, reading-fee policy, and representative titles that the agency sold. Herman's *Guide* includes a Q&A that provides insights into the agents. Some of the questions are: What are the common mistakes most authors make? What can writers do to enhance their chances of getting you as their agent? and What do you think about editors? The *Guide* also profiles publishers and a good number of articles by industry insiders.

The Writer's Market, by Kathryn S. Brogan, Robert Lee Brewer (Writer's Digest Books, published annually). This book gives contact information, some brief background on agents, and the percentage of fiction, nonfiction, scholarly, reference, children's books, and so forth that the agency handles. For some agencies, it lists the percentage of clients who are "new/unpublished." The types of book the agency handles, specialty areas, recent sales, terms, and writers' conferences may also be included. The listing also may state what an agency is "seeking" and describe the type of submissions it welcomes.

Guide to Literary Agents (Writer's Digest Books, published annually). This guidebook's introductory section includes a number of helpful articles. Markets are broken down into literary agents, script agents, production companies, script contests, independent publicists, and writers' conferences. For literary agencies, this guide gives contact information, brief background, who the agency represents, and its areas of specialization, which may list what the firm is "seeking." It also lists submission requirements, recent sales, terms, and tips.

The Literary Market Place: The Directory of the American Book Publishing Industry With Industry Yellow Pages (Information Today, Inc., published annually). Literary Market Place is less detailed than other guidebooks. It lists when an agency was founded and the types of books it handles. It also may give the submission requirements and whether unsolicited submissions are accepted, if a reading fee is charged, and if foreign rights are covered. The listing may include titles recently placed and memberships.

Everyone Who's Anyone in Adult Trade Publishing and Tinseltown Too, by Gerard Jones, searchable online directory at *http://everyone whosanyone.com*.

"In researching agencies, don't just rely on one directory because different directories contain different information," agent Michael Larsen advises. "For example, Jeff Herman's guide asks agents questions that enable readers to get a great sense of the agents' personalities and what they're like. While Writer's Digest's *Guide to Literary Agents* contains the most exhaustive list of subjects that agencies handle."

The agents who choose not to be listed in directories want only referrals from their clients and contacts; they want some personal recommendation from people who know them, not cold contacts. These

Rick Says

"Although the guides can be an invaluable resource, all agents are not listed in all guides. Some agents restrict their listings to particular guides, and others prefer not to be listed in any. In fact, some go to great lengths to have their names removed from certain, if not all, directories."

agents believe personal referrals boost the quality of the submissions they receive and reduce the number of dead-end inquiries they get.

Network

Since writing can be such a solitary activity, it's imperative that writers get outside input and broaden their horizons. Spend time with others who have had the same problems and speak the same language.

Meet and talk with other writers: Join writers' groups, including those online. Attend conferences, workshops, and seminars and take courses. Befriend other writers and people who work in all aspects of the industry; become a member of writers' communities. The writers you meet may have, or know others who have, agents you can contact.

Expanding your contacts will help you to focus and improve the quality of your writing. It can also assist you in finding resources, including editors, illustrators, designers, publicists, and agents. Agents will be more receptive to you when people they know and respect recommend you.

To find an agent, start by sending out feelers.

- Contact everyone you know and tell them that you are trying to obtain information about literary agents.
- Ask if they know agents, writers, or people who work in publishing—anyone who could help.
- Approach everyone, your friends and family, work and business associates, your doctor, clergy, attorney, and accountant.
- Speak with people who work at local bookstores, libraries, and newspapers. Spread a wide net.
- Be patient and persistent. Keep asking, and follow up on every lead.
- Pursue any lead that might help you connect with an agent no matter how many steps it may take or remote it may seem.

When you contact people who could help, immediately tell them who referred you to them. Write the name of the person who referred you in the subject line of your e-mail or put it up front in your letter or phone message. For example, write or say, "David Lees suggested you might be able to help me find a literary agent for my book *Writers' Block*."

If you reach writers or people who know writers, explain your situation. Writers understand; they've been through it and they know how hard it is to find an agent and get published. Most will be happy to help.

However, most won't recommend you blindly; they will want to know something about you and see your writing. So be prepared. Have something solid written about your project and yourself. Offer to immediately send it, which will demonstrate that you're professional and prepared. This will give your contacts more confidence in passing your material on.

Another networking approach is to read the acknowledgments of books you admire or feel are similar to yours. Then contact the authors and tell them about your book. Tell them about your project and ask them questions or for advice. Try to build a relationship. Many authors will be responsive and try to help. Many authors won't respond, but others may. They know the problems writers face and may be willing to help. Plus, they may like or identify with you and your ideas.

You can also attend talks and book signings by writers you admire and try to speak with them. Many hang around at the end of events and are happy to talk. Have your pitch ready so you can tell them about your project clearly and succinctly. Understand that they may be tired, so be respectful of their time. Have a written description of your work on hand that you can give them or offer to send.

Attend workshops, seminars, and conferences. Agents are fixtures at many writers' conferences, so these events can be great places to meet and connect with them. For information on writers' conferences see *Writer's Digest* (*www.writersdigest.com*) and ShawGuides (*http://writing. shawguides.com*).

Research Agents

Now it's time to turn your attention to specific agents. You can obtain information on them from:

- Similar books to your own
- The Internet
- Networking
- Attending writers' organization conferences, workshops, meetings, and classes
- The Association of Authors' Representatives (AAR)
- Guidebooks and online guides

To find names of agents who could be good for you, leaf through books that are similar to yours. Search bookstores, libraries, and online booksellers. If you can't find other publications directly on point or somewhat close, broaden your search to see who published books on the same or related subjects. When you find similar books, read the acknowledgments to find whom the authors thanked. Authors usually state their appreciation of their agents in their books' acknowledgments section.

"If a writer has no clue of what agent to approach, the guidebooks won't offer much initial help," Santa Monica agent Bonnie Solow warns. "Go to the bookshelf and find books that you consider kindred spirits. Typically, authors will have acknowledged their agents in their books. Then research them."

Check the guidebooks and agents' Web sites. Look up agents, note the areas in which they specialize, and the types of properties they accept. If they handle your topic, place their names on a list. Verify their contact information and carefully note the correct spelling of the names of those you plan to contact.

Don't forget that reference guidebooks are published annually. So make sure to use the latest, most current edition because agents frequently move and guidebooks quickly get out of date. Be especially wary of the volumes in local libraries because they are often ancient.

You can search agents online by their names. Go ahead and Google them. Read profiles, articles, or stories about them. Check out interviews they gave or quotes or excerpts from their speeches. Find out who they are, what their tastes are, what they believe, and what they look for from writers.

When you contact them, reference information that you found in your research. For example, "I loved _____, which you represented" or "I loved what you said about integrity in *Details* magazine." Show them that you've done your homework, you know about them, and you are specifically targeting them because you think that they could be the ideal agent for you.

Some sources are not neutral. They may state that an agent is "not recommended" or give information indicating that the agents have been accused of engaging in questionable practices. Although we can't guarantee the accuracy of all their information, such sources may help you in making a decision. These include:

- *Editors & Preditors*, a searchable online directory at *www. anotherealm.com/prededitors*. Although it provides little more than contact information, many of the entries are linked to the agents' Web sites. For some entries, this directory states that reading fees are charged, conflicts exist, and whether they are recommended or not recommended.
- The Science Fiction Writer's Association's Writer Beware (at *www.sfwa.org/beware/agents.html*) maintains a database that contains information on more than 300 agents who may engage in questionable practices. Writers can send SFWA the names of agents and it will send them summaries of the data in its files.
- Agent Research & Evaluation (*www.agentresearch.com*), which also collects writers' complaints, offers a free agent verification service.

■ Google Groups (*http://groups.google.com*) has a searchable database of Usenet messages where writers may have posted questions about agents. To find information, enter the agent's name in the search box. If an agent has a common name, include the words "literary agent."

Literary agencies usually post their submission requirements on their Web sites. Generally, they identify the subjects they accept and those they don't handle, the items you should submit and those not to submit. If you want an agency to consider representing you, follow its guidelines—to the letter!

Agents constantly complained to us that most inquiries they receive are on subjects that they don't handle. They also said that despite specifically instructing writers to send them only query letters or e-mails, they routinely received packages containing proposals, sample chapters, entire manuscripts, and additional material about the authors or their projects.

"Before you contact any agent, go to his or her Web site and look at the sales he or she made in the past," agent Sharlene Martin suggests. "See if he or she has done books on or close to your topic. Check the books that the agent is currently offering and you'll see that there is a consistency to the type of books the agent responds to."

The fact that writers don't follow agencies' specific instructions automatically disqualifies them as agency clients. So, take what agencies say as gospel if you want to get your foot in the door.

Keep Records

Compile a list of potential publishers and/or agents to contact. Before you submit a proposal or a query letter, learn what each will accept and how each wishes to receive it. Note the information you obtain on a contact list as follows.

AGENT CONTACT LIST

Name and Firm	Specialties	Contact Information	Submission Requirements
Jeffrey Long, The Literary Group	Fiction, memoirs, short stories	xxxx@x.com 555-555-1161	Postal query letter, first 15 manuscript pages, SASE
Marjie Turell, The Mema Agency	Art and design	xxxx@x.com 555-555-5151	Query letter, samples of art
Doug Devon, Creative Literary	Mystery, science fiction, suspense	xxxx@x.com 555-555-4567	Query letter, excellent credentials, bio, SASE
Marcy O'Dawd, O'Dawd Agency	Children's books	xxxx@x.com 555-555-2121	Query letter, sample chapter, sample illustrations

It's perfectly acceptable for writers to submit their work to more than one agent at a time. However, industry protocol calls for them to inform all the agents that they have made submissions to the others. When writers agree to be represented by an agent, they should inform all the other agents they have approached.

Maintaining a contact list will help you to be well organized. It will make it easier for you to give publishers and agents exactly what they require in the precise format they want and to inform them that you decided to sign with another firm.

A contact list will also form the basis for a log on which you should track the submissions you send. Your submission log should include:

1. The names of those you sent submissions to
2. The date each submission was sent
3. The responses you received
4. Any follow-up requirements

SUBMISSION LOG

Name	Firm	Date Sent	Response	Follow Up
Jeffrey Long	The Literary Group	11/17/05	Send proposal	Sent 1/7/06
Marjie Turell	The Mema Agency	11/17/05	Not interested	
Doug Devon	Creative Literary	11/20/05	Wants exclusive	Decide & contact by 1/10/06
Don Dontalone	Big Books	11/20/05	No response	

As we've noted, many publishers and agents do not accept unsolicited submissions, including query letters. However, those that do usually provide clear submission guidelines on their sites. If unsolicited materials are accepted, identify exactly what material they want, the format they prefer, and the address where your submission should be sent.

An Agent's View

"I like to see that the author has done the necessary homework to know a little about us and what kind of properties we prefer to represent," Ron Laitsch (*www.authenticcreations.com*) of the Authentic Creations Literary Agency, Inc., in Lawrenceville, Georgia, points out. "Something original always catches my interest. If the format of the letter has been copied from some source, it reads like so many others we see. With over 200 queries a week, we need something that makes the letter stand out. Some are clever and make us laugh, while others get to the point with information about the book. The author should always include something about his or her qualifications to write the book, including background information about any previously published materials. Something about our agency always makes us feel that the author has at least looked at our background to see if we might be a good fit for the author's work."

Build a Platform

When editors consider buying a book, a major factor in their decision is whether the author has the ability and commitment to energetically publicize and promote the book. Editors want authors who have strong platforms: followings, supporters, and fans who will buy their books.

Since platforms have become so critical in publishing, the best advice we can give you is to build one ASAP. The more of a platform you have in place when you contact agents, the greater your chances of success. The big problem in building a platform is that it takes time.

Most writers don't learn that they need a platform until they hear it from agents and editors. At that point, they can't simply pick up the phone or make a wish and—presto!—they're on *Oprah*. We'll discuss platforms in more depth in Chapter 11, "Why Agents Love Platforms."

Web Sites

To be a successful writer in today's market, you should build a strong Internet presence. "We are moving into a visually, graphically active, interactive world through the Internet, television, games, cell phones, and Amazon," Richard Curtis explains. "When I pitch authors to editors over the phone, I can actually hear them typing on the keyboard as we speak. I know that while we're talking, they are going on Google or Amazon and checking out the author. They'll say, 'I see, oh yeah, I see the author's picture or the cover of his last five books.' So, if that's what editors now do in order to identify a writer and place him or her in a context that they feel comfortable with, let's give it to them."

The trick, according to Curtis, is to create a presence or the appearance of a platform that editors can easily find and with which they can relate. So he starts by working with his clients to create impressive Web sites, which he believes are imperative for authors in today's interactive world.

How writers present themselves and the information they provide on their sites can be revealing for agents and editors. Since we're living in an increasingly electronic world, editors can refer others in the acquisition process to a writer's Web site for information that may impact the decision on whether or not to buy a book.

In this electronic age, having a top-notch Web site shows that a writer is professional. Increasingly, editors are viewing them as tickets to the game.

If you're a nonfiction writer and have a certain expertise, you need a Web site even if it doesn't reach many people. The Web site is critical because it gives you a presence in the market that publishers can easily access and see. When you have a Web site, it can help an editor sell your proposal because it provides information about you: that you are an expert who has a following; that your site gets 1,000 hits a month; that you lead an active chat group, have a newsletter that reaches thousands, and have written articles and conducted workshops and seminars.

You should also develop reciprocal links with other Web sites. Links from other Web sites will bring you additional visitors, and those from your site to other sites can help your visitors get more information. Be discriminating and link up with only the best, because connections with authoritative sites that get lots of hits will boost your status as an expert. Links with lesser sites will place you in bad company.

Be Ready

You never know when you will receive requests for submissions from agents or people who can reach them; they can come out of the blue. Long after you queried an agent, after months with no word, you could finally be asked to submit a proposal and/or a portion of your work. You might bump into an old friend who is now a writer and has a great agent. So you better be ready!

When their moments come, many writers can't deliver; they can't make the most of their opportunities, opportunities that other writers would kill for. So seize the opportunity when it arises because it may not come again. Here are some steps to follow:

1. Have your proposal written and ready to go the moment an agent shows interest. When many writers get submission requests, they just go back and throw together a proposal or fix up one they previously sent that was rejected. Or, they feverishly try to work on and improve the sample chapters the agent requested. Don't fall into that trap. Before you contact agents, write your book proposal. Have the entire proposal finished and then polish, refine, and buff it until it glows.

2. Ask your friends or colleagues to read and criticize it. Ask teachers, writers, editors, or others who know writing to review your proposal for spelling, grammar, and punctuation errors.

3. If your friends and contacts can't review your work, ask if they know any professional editors. Get the names of editors from local writing clubs or organizations or from the staff at bookstores or libraries. Then have your proposal professionally reviewed.

4. When an agent shows interest, make sure that you fully understand exactly what he or she wants. See that every detail has been checked and that the proposal contains exactly what the agent wants. If your proposal isn't in the form requested or it doesn't contain everything the agent requested, promptly fix it, give it a final check, and ship it out. Send it by return mail or electronically, however the agent requests.

5. Promptly sending a dazzling, high-caliber proposal will impress an agent. It will show that you're prepared, professional, and passionate about your book.

Your Opening Pitch

YOUR FIRST CONTACT WITH AN AGENT IS CRITICAL.

The lesson that your parents and teachers drummed into you about the importance of making good first impressions is true. First impressions really make a difference, and they make a difference with agents whether they're verbal or written!

Agents are extremely busy, so approach them as if they have short attention spans. They're also keen judges who will examine you and your pitch from the first word.

- Know exactly what you want to say.
- Be brief.
- Get right to the point.
- Be unmistakably clear in telling them about your proposed book.

To prepare for your initial contact, write a list of the important factors you want to convey. Start by listing key words that represent your ideas. Then, express each of your most important ideas in a few sentences.

The essential questions that those few sentences should answer are:

1. What is your book about? Describe its idea or concept. Will it teach, show, explain, describe, illustrate, or question?
2. Who will your book benefit? Specifically name the group or audience it will reach and, if possible, its size.
3. How will your book benefit them? State exactly what they will gain from your book.
4. Why are you qualified to write this book? Blow your own horn here, but make beautiful music, not a raucous blare.

Okay, we know that all this information seems like a lot to stuff into just a few sentences, but that's the task; that's the exercise that you have to complete so that you can concisely, but clearly, describe your book. That's your job!

Work on it; it will probably take some time. Boil down the answers to the above questions to two or three sentences that you can recite in ten to fifteen seconds. Make sure that you include all your most important points.

The easiest way to proceed may be to write down the answers to the four questions above and blend them into two sentences. Don't worry about their length or your grammar. Just be sure that they contain the answers to each of the four questions. Concentrate on including all of the descriptive content.

Reread each sentence and refine it by substituting more graphic, colorful, or expressive words. Circle and delete all words that are not essential. Then read the sentences aloud; listen to their flow and trust your ear. Keep reciting your sentences aloud and see if you can eliminate other extraneous, unnecessary words.

Test various versions out on your family and friends. Often, what you think is perfectly clear will mean something entirely different to others. Get their input and make appropriate changes in accordance with their suggestions. Make sure that your message is clear.

Recite your pitch frequently to yourself until you feel completely comfortable reciting it. Then write the final version. Underline three

Robyn Says

"In writing your opening pitch, focus first on being clear and precise. It's important to get to the point and avoid boasting or trying to be too clever, cool, or witty—unless, of course, that's the subject of your book. Don't let anything divert the listener's attention or obscure the message you want to convey. Above all, make your pitch clear and easily understandable. The last thing you want to do is to communicate in a way that prevents listeners from instantly understanding what you're saying. At the most, authors have only a few moments to make a fabulous first impression, so focus on your message and present your credentials in the most persuasive way."

or four words that express the most important information you want to communicate. Close your eyes and picture them; make a mental note of them and stress them when you recite your pitch.

Let's examine some opening pitches:

Pitch #1: "Would you be interested in my book, *PR Express*, which teaches nonprofit organizations how to expertly and inexpensively run in-house publicity campaigns?"

This pitch is direct, simple, and brief. It wastes no time in telling the agent the name of the book and that it will show nonprofits how to run their own PR campaigns. It also points out that the book has been written for and will benefit nonprofit organizations by teaching them how to proficiently and inexpensively get publicity.

The author's qualifications can be addressed subsequently in a single sentence as follows: "In fifteen years with the PubPub, an international public relations firm, I have run hundreds of innovative publicity campaigns for nonprofit corporations."

Pitch #2: "I am the head of cardiology for a national hospital chain. Would you be interested in my book, *Ticker Tastes: Heart Healthy Recipes from a Top Cardiologist Chef?*"

This pitch leads off with the author's strongest asset, her credentials: that she is the top heart expert for a major health-care group. Her qualifications alone will get an agent's attention. Then she gives her book's title to explain what her book is about—providing heart-healthy recipes. Through the title, she also explains that she is a chef.

Pitch #3: "Over 90 percent of individual taxpayers overlook numerous deductions that they can legally take. My book, *The Top 100 Tax Deductions People Miss*, will show readers, in easy-to-understand language, how to stop throwing away their money."

Facts and statistics, especially when they're shocking, grab a reader's attention. And they can be even more potent when they're about health, money, or sex. If you have shocking or surprising data, use it.

Similarly, state the size or the buying power of your audience. If you are a recognizable celebrity, are an authority in your field, have written prior books, appear regularly on TV or radio, or write a regular column, say so right up front.

Hone your opening pitch so that every word counts. Keep it brief, clear and direct. Remember, screeners usually must convey your message to others, so make it easy to grasp so the right information gets passed on.

Be prepared to follow your initial pitch with an extended version that takes no more than twenty to thirty seconds to deliver. Your follow-up should expand upon your opening pitch or add important new information that wasn't included. Also be ready to answer questions.

Expectations

Clarify your own expectations. Have a good idea of exactly what you would like an agent to do for you. For example, you would like him to sign you with a large, well-known publisher and obtain at least a $30,000 advance. Then ask yourself if you're being realistic.

It's important for agents and their clients to know each other's expectations. Making expectations clear facilitates good communication and helps ensure that you're both on the same page.

Agent Bonnie Solow of Santa Monica, California, tries to learn what writers expect before they agree to work together, so she makes it a point to ask potential clients early in the game, usually during their first conversation. If someone says, "I've had five agents. They all were terrible, but I hear you're wonderful," then Solow smells trouble.

Solow also asks potential clients what they expect financially. The expectations of one prospective client were so outrageous that he told her his book would be "bigger than the Bible."

"Grounding authors' unrealistic expectations" is a big part of New Jersey agent John Willig's work. "The notion that when a writer gets a big advance it will ensure that he or she will have a good publishing experience or success is total nonsense," Willig says. He also notes that he has never attended a sales or marketing meeting, after a book was sold, in which anyone brought up the advance. "They are not influenced by the amount of the author's advance. The sales and marketing people don't give a damn about the author's advance; all they care about is how this book is going to make the company or them personally more money, so they can look good within the company."

Professionals prefer to deal with informed clients; it makes their jobs easier because they don't have to explain every little point. When clients bring knowledge to the table, it lifts the level of the client/agent relationship and they can usually have a more efficient and productive relationship.

Action Steps

1. What three things must writers do before contacting an agent?
2. Describe how to network to get agents' names.
3. What sources should writers use to research agents?
4. What information should a writer's agent submission list contain?
5. Write an opening pitch that you could deliver to an agent.

Remember:

 Finding the right agent takes time, work, and effort. Develop a detailed plan of attack before you start and then stick with it. Make your search a separate project distinct from the writing of your book. Give it your full attention and gather plenty of information so you can find the right agent.

 Educate yourself about the literary agency business. Then identify and research specific agents. Create an agent contact list and keep records on whom you contacted, when you contacted him or her, and his or her responses. Build your platform, start a Web site, and have your proposal ready to submit. Then you will be ready to send query letters or e-mails. Prepare for your initial contact by planning how to tell agents what your book is about, who will benefit from it, how they will benefit, and why you're so qualified to write it.

CHAPTER

7

"Thunder is good, thunder is impressive: But it is lightning that does the work."

Mark Twain

Query Letters and E-mail

THIS CHAPTER WILL COVER:

▶ Putting it in writing
▶ Query basics
▶ Query length
▶ Query content
▶ Sample query
▶ Before it mails
▶ Responses

THE FIRST HURDLE that writers must clear is getting an agent to show interest in their work . . . and that hurdle is quite high! Fortunately, writers can initially reach agents in a number of ways, including through referrals, meeting them at conferences and events, and sending them queries. For both fiction and nonfiction, most initial contacts are made via queries, and the majority of queries are now made by e-mail.

Agents are swamped with inquiries from writers. Agents informed us that they receive hundreds of queries from would-be authors every week. To handle the flow, most have surrounded themselves with screening mechanisms that would make the Secret Service proud. Inquiries must go through well-trained screeners, and reaching the agent can be very challenging.

Many agents won't take telephone inquiries. Unless one of their clients, relatives, or close personal friends recommends you, many agents won't take your call.

Put It in Writing

Regardless of how you connect with an agent or who recommended you, the agent will invariably ask you to send him or her something in writing. The major exception is big-name celebrities.

Since agents deal in writing, it's essential for them to see how well you write before they give you any more of their precious time. So most insist that you send them written queries, and many have formal guidelines that they expect you to follow. Check their Web sites and see exactly what they want.

That said, every rule has its exception. Some agents, including some big and highly respected agents, do accept telephone inquiries. However, they, too, have screeners who may put you through the third degree and make you regret not sending a query letter. Before you contact an agent, be prepared and know exactly what you plan to say so that the right message gets to the agent.

Query Basics

A query letter or e-mail can be the most important thing a writer ever writes. If a query doesn't do its job, a writer probably will never have a shot at publishing his or her book. We can't overstate the importance of query letters!

"A query letter should be the soul of the writer coming out in its absolute best form," according to agent Sharlene Martin. "You don't get a second chance with an agent, so they must be fashioned in a way that's attention getting without being too gimmicky. An author must say what the book is, who he or she is, and what he or she has to contribute on that subject matter."

Literary agents want query letters or e-mails that describe:

1. What your book is about.
2. Who your book will benefit.

3. How large that group is.
4. How your book will benefit them.
5. Why you are qualified to write this book.

Frequently, agents will refer you to their Web sites, where their submission requirements are posted. San Francisco agent and author Michael Larsen, of the Larsen-Pomada Literary Agency, takes an interesting and somewhat unusual approach. He requests that potential clients send him two items: (1) the title of their book and (2) a promotion plan that follows the requirements on the Larsen-Pomada Web site. "Those two pieces of information alone will enable me to determine whether I can sell the book to a big house."

Some Query Letter Don'ts

When you submit your query to a literary agent, DON'T:

- Send submissions for books on topics they don't handle.
- Address the submission generally, such as to "Dear Agent" or "To Whom It May Concern."
- Misspell the agent or agency's name.
- Include any typos, cross-outs, or misspellings.
- Send your manuscript or parts of it.
- Send your book proposal.
- Send your press package, clippings, or other promotional info.
- Blow your own horn; instead, let your submission do it.
- Omit the self-addressed stamped envelope (SASE).
- Call to see if it arrived or to try to sell you or your book.

What Good Query Letters Can Do

A good query letter shows agents that you:

- Have a good idea for a salable book that is compatible with their interests.
- Can express yourself clearly in writing.

Robyn Says

"The primary purpose of a query letter is to ask if an agent or editor is interested in learning more about your book. A query letter is your opening shot, so take careful aim and take your best shot. A query letter usually conveys the first impression of you and your book that an agent will receive. Like most first impressions, it can be critical . . . so make it memorable! Capture the agent's interest by clearly demonstrating that you're professional, disciplined, and articulate. Communicate that you have a great idea for a book that will sell."

- Have the ability and qualifications to complete and promote your book.
- Are professional.

On receiving your query letter, agents will make a quick assessment of you and your professionalism. If queries come in colorful packages; are printed on overly decorative stationery; have flowery stamps; contain cross-outs, typos, or misspellings; or have a generally sloppy appearance, recipients will label you unprofessional. If they don't reject your submission, they will probably delay reading it or assign it to an underling. To make a strong initial impression, submit a professional-looking query letter!

Professional-looking query letters:

- Are written on business-type letterhead that clearly gives your name and contact information.
- Stick to basic white or off-white 8½- by 11-inch paper and use a standard typeface that can be read easily.
- Don't get fancy or, worse yet, cute.
- Avoid bold colors, gimmicky borders, or other features that could distract from your message.

■ Include a SASE with the proper amount of postage if you want anything back.

In query letters, strive for brevity and clarity. Make your letters short, well written, and to the point. Your main objective is to get your foot in the door, to grab an agent's interest, and make him or her ask for more information about your book. The best way to do so is to clearly and professionally communicate the specialness of your book idea in plain, straightforward, easily understood English.

What Turns Agents Off

"An immediate turn-off is when I receive an inquiry that shows that the writer hasn't done enough research," agent Edward Knappman reports. "If I get an inquiry regarding a novel, it's obvious that they haven't done enough research to learn that we don't handle fiction. If they haven't researched our agency, the first thing I ask is, 'How can they do enough research for the book?'"

Another instant turn-off occurs when the agent's name or the firm's name is misspelled. Remarkably, agents informed us that such misspellings are common.

"An e-mail query should follow all of the protocols of a professionally typewritten letter. It should be neat, correctly spelled, and grammatically correct," agent Sharlene Martin advises. "E-mail in our pop-culture world has become an informal method of communication, but e-mail queries should not be informal. E-mail shorthand in a query is not appropriate. A query must be professional, and addressed to a particular person. Don't send it as a mass e-mail that shows the addresses of everyone to whom it was sent."

"A query must describe the big picture or give a clear overview instead of giving every detail that's in the book," New York agent Liv Bloomer, of the Bloomer Literary Agency, points out. "In every step of the life of a book, there are a couple of dozen people who have to sell it to somebody, and the message gets watered down as it passes from sales hand to sales hand: the person selling to the bookstores, the person selling to foreign publishers, whoever it may be. If the message can't be delivered clearly and briefly, someone is going to get it wrong. And by the end, it doesn't resemble your book anymore."

Query Length

For nonfiction books, try to keep query letters to a single page, but never exceed two pages. Always include all your contact information and a self-addressed stamped envelope. When you can clearly describe your project in one page, you demonstrate to agents that you can write.

For fictional works, include a synopsis of your book that runs a few double-spaced pages. Offer to forward the manuscript if it's completed. If the manuscript has not been completed, offer to send sample chapters.

If you send an e-mail query, write no more than a single screen. Don't send e-mail attachments unless you're specifically asked to, because they probably won't be opened. Use the same high standards for e-mail queries that you use for hard-copy submissions because agents will judge them with equal severity.

In some agencies, e-mail queries face more challenges than postal mail submissions. They are reviewed by a number of screeners and must be outstanding to reach the decision maker. Conversely, postal mail queries that are addressed to the decision maker usually travel a shorter, less-arduous route before they get through.

Query letters stand a good chance of being read simply because they're short. Conversely, they run the risk of being skimmed or even disregarded if they're long. So craft your query letters carefully and make them brief. If agents are interested, they will request more information.

Feel free to send query letters to more than one agent at a time; agents simultaneously send proposals to multiple publishers. If an agent

"When you forward query letters to agents, direct them to specific individuals, not to an unnamed "Gentleman," "Dear Sir or Madam" or the like. Some literary agencies are large, so imprecisely addressed mailings can easily get lost.

"When you don't address your query to a specific person, it indicates that you haven't researched the agency and the individual agents. Many agents will take this as an indication that you don't have the qualities required to write and promote a successful book."

shows interest and requests a proposal or manuscript, he or she may also ask for the exclusive right to read or sell your book. If you agree to a reading exclusive, make it for a short term—not longer than a month or six weeks. An exclusive agreement for an agent to sell your work should be in writing and should be cancelable by either party by giving written notice.

Query Content

A nonfiction query letter must include:

1. *A tight lead sentence that describes your book.* The lead sentence should be a grabber or a hook that excites readers and makes them want to read further. So sculpt your lead artfully. Give the title, length, and what the book is about. Questions/answers, statistics, and anecdotes can also make effective opening sentences. Keep your lead to two or two and a half lines. If you need to round off your lead or to add other crucial information that didn't fit in your lead, add another short sentence, but don't exceed a line or two. If you have celebrity status, work it into the lead or second sentence.

2. *A paragraph or two supporting and amplifying the lead.* This paragraph should:
   a. Provide more details on:
      - The subject of the book.
      - Why your book is special or how it differs from other books.
      - The market for the book.
      - How it's organized, designed, or formatted and its page count.
      - Why it will interest editors.
   b. Point out problems that your book will solve and concrete ways that it will help readers.
   c. Include facts or statistics that show the size of your book's potential market.
   d. State whether the manuscript has been written or when you expect to complete it.
3. *Your biography.* Don't just use your standard resume or simply stress your educational and business background; instead, show why you're uniquely qualified to write this book. Summarize your hands-on experience. Include your past writing credits, awards in your field, and platform.
4. *A summary statement.* Thank the recipient for his or her time and offer to send additional materials such as a proposal, sample chapters, or the manuscript.

Remember that in a query letter, brevity and clarity are essential. Don't stuff your query letter mailings with other materials such as your table of contents, sample chapters, or loads of biographical information. Bulky packages may not be opened. Instead, offer to send a proposal containing those items and enclose a self-addressed stamped envelope.

Be Direct, Clear, and Concise

According to agents, when the concept of the book you propose is strong, you should get right to it; don't hesitate or waste time. Tell the agent about it immediately. Clearly explain what your book is about right up front in order to grab the agent's interest.

In a query, clarity comes first. Your primary purpose is to convince agents that you have an outstanding book idea that you can clearly express. Agents want clarity; they won't waste their time on writers when they can't figure out what they're trying to say.

Concentrate on vividly describing your book idea and its market before you try to demonstrate your wit, intelligence, or writing skill. Communicate; don't showboat.

Query letters that are written on a writer's letterhead and give the writer's name in the opening sentence turn off New York City agent Liv Bloomer. "It happens all the time. Although the writer's name and address are at the top, the first line of the letter says, 'Hello, my name is _____.' Then they also give their name at the bottom. Telling me their name three times prejudices me because it wastes time. If you follow the rule of thumb that you have only a page to make your pitch, why waste any of it unnecessarily repeating your name?"

A Sample Query

Let's examine the structure and elements in the sample query below. It's direct, to the point, and has no frills. It starts by baiting the hook with statistics that show that a problem exists. Then, it states that the book will provide information that can prevent that problem, and it highlights with bullet points the specific benefits it will contain. The query next devotes a paragraph to describing the book's market and another to giving the author's qualifications and platform.

Finally, the query concludes by thanking the agent for considering the project and hoping that they can work together. The sample query follows.

November 17, 2005
Ms. A. Agent
A to Z Literary Agency
Jersey City, NJ 07301

Dear Ms. _____ ,

Employment-related lawsuits account for twenty-five percent of the cases brought in federal courts. Employers lose roughly two out of three cases that go to trial and that's not counting those that are settled out of court. In California, the average wrongful termination jury award is $1.3 million and employers still have to shell out an average of $450,000 per suit in legal expenses.

Ironically, suits by ex-employees are preventable, but many employers don't know what to do. My book, *How to Fire Employees Without Getting Sued*, provides the answers. It explains in clear, direct, and easily understood nontechnical language exactly what employers can do to stay out of court. This book:

- Explains the basic principles of employee termination law in clear terms that nonattorneys can easily understand.
- Shows the value of adopting and implementing a comprehensive approach for dealing with personnel from hiring through firing.
- Points out the advantages of requiring the use of nonjudicial alternatives for workplace disputes.
- Teaches employers how to anticipate and avoid potential workplace problems.
- Provides practical and proven solutions to resolve workplace problems before they cost employers a fortune.
- Includes easy-to-follow forms that employers can adapt for their businesses.

The primary market for *How to Fire Employees* is the over 4 million small-business operators that employ less than ten people and do not have in-house personnel or human resource departments. The information in this book will also appeal to larger businesses and individual operators who are thinking about hiring an employee.

As a practicing attorney and published author who has helped clients to avoid and defend against wrongful termination suits for over fifteen years, I feel well qualified to write this book. I have coauthored two previous books and I regularly speak and conduct workshops on employment law. My monthly column appears in the Gazette Syndicate Features News publications, and I have been the subject of frequent coverage by the national and local media. I will vigorously promote *How to Fire Employees* to make it a huge success.

Thank you for considering *How to Fire Employees*. I hope that you will be interested in representing me.

Sincerely,

_____

Before It Mails

Carefully proofread everything you send. Typos, misspellings, and grammatical mistakes are the kiss of death. So are sloppy-looking submissions that have spots, smudges, stains, creases, or cross-outs. Focus on showing that you're an accomplished, professional writer whom the publisher or agent can trust. Check each letter or e-mail query by doing the following:

1. Let it sit overnight after you complete it, and then print it out the following day when you can read it with refreshed eyes. If you make changes the next day, hold it to reread for one additional day.
2. Have a reliable copyeditor read it.

3. Send every e-mail query letter to yourself, printing it out the next day and then reading it before you send it to agents or editors. Make your final read from a hard-copy printout, not the computer screen.

4. Don't forget to include a SASE if you want anything to be returned, and make sure it has sufficient postage.

5. If you submit a query via postal mail or a delivery service, check whether the agent has any objection to your requiring a signature. Some agents hate having to sign for submissions because if they miss them, it can be a hassle to get packages or call for redelivery. However, if the agent has no objection, request a signature acknowledging delivery because mail can go astray.

Some E-mail Don'ts

If you submit via e-mail, don't use informal e-mail conventions and abbreviations. Use the same high standard you would for business letters. Make it the same quality as a letter for a job, which it just may be. Many agents don't understand e-mail jargon and others may be turned off by it or consider it unprofessional.

Don't e-mail submissions that you have not fully read and double-checked for grammar, punctuation, spelling, and proper structure. When you edit on a computer screen, it can be easy to miss errors, so print a hard copy of the query and read it carefully before you hit send.

Responses

Query letters give agents an opportunity to comment on your project and give you constructive feedback. Savvy agents know the market and can suggest slants or directions that can improve your book and the chances of its selling. In addition, it's easier for many writers to accept feedback at the query-letter stage than it is after they have written an extensive proposal, chapters, or even an entire manuscript.

If agents are interested in your query, they will probably respond to you within a few weeks. Don't badger them, call, write, or send e-mail asking whether they received your letter for sixty days. Then write either a brief inquiry note or an e-mail.

Resist the temptation to call an agent to ask if your query arrived. If you need assurances, a return receipt should do the job. Then, just try to be patient.

When writers call to inquire whether their submissions have arrived, agents and their staff don't react favorably. They know from experience that these calls are often just ruses that writers concoct to speak with an agent and try to convince him or her to represent them.

Also don't send agents stuff at a later date that you forgot to include with your query, or that you think might influence their decision. Just wait, and if you get no response within a month, move on.

Action Steps

1. Name five things you should not do when you send or e-mail a query to an agent.
2. How long should a query letter or e-mail be?
3. Name the four elements that should be included in a query letter or e-mail.
4. What steps should you take before you send your query?
5. How long should you wait before you contact an agent who has not responded to your query?

Remember:

 Agents are swamped with inquiries from writers; many receive hundreds of queries each week. Many agents won't take telephone inquiries; they usually want you to send query letters or e-mails to see if they are interested in handling your book. Since literary agents deal in writing, they will probably ask you to send them something in writing. The major exception is big-name celebrities.

 Queries should state what your book is about, whom it will benefit, the size of target audiences, how the book will benefit them, and why you are qualified to write it. Keep your query to a single page; include all your contact information and a self-addressed stamped envelope. Carefully proofread everything you send, and don't bug agents if you don't get a quick response.

CHAPTER
8

"Times are bad. Children no longer obey their parents, and everyone is writing a book."

Cicero

Reports from the Trenches

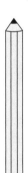

THIS CHAPTER WILL COVER:

■ What agents say about queries and e-mails

NOW THAT YOU'VE READ about query letters and e-mails, we thought that you would like a sampling of what agents have to say on the subject. So, in gathering information for this book, we asked agents the following question:

> *Could you describe one submission that you received from a writer, either in an initial query or a proposal, that really grabbed you and explain why and how it captured your interest?*

Here are some of the responses we received in literary agents' own words.

›› PAMELA BRODOWSKY

International Literary Arts, LLC

E-mail: *query@InternationalLiteraryArts.com*

www.InternationalLiteraryArts.com

Above all else in both query letters and proposals, I first look to the author's writing skills and next the credentials. Who is the author, what has he done, and what can he do?

One fictional query that stood out to me immediately was headed with a fictitious *New York Times* headline. It was meant as an attention grabber—and it did just that.

›› SHEREE BYKOFSKY AND JANET ROSEN

Sheree Bykofsky Associates, Inc.

16 West 36th Street, 13th Floor

New York, NY 10018

One submission that really grabbed and captured our interest was the proposal that eventually was sold as *Lapsing Into a Comma: A Curmudgeon's Guide to the Many Things That Can Go Wrong in Print—and How to Avoid Them*, by Bill Walsh (McGraw-Hill).

This erudite and amusing guide to copyediting and language usage fulfilled all of the requirements we look for in this kind of nonfiction. The author had excellent credentials (he had a popular and funny copyediting Web site and worked at the *Washington Post*). The writing was stylish and distinctive; he provided a point of view and gave the reader useful information, as well. Even though there are many other books on usage, this project showed how it was needed in a crowded market. And it showed us with great intelligence and flair.

Lapsing Into a Comma sold well enough and enjoyed enough critical praise for the publisher to follow up with Walsh's wonderful sequel, *Elephants of Style: A Trunkload of Tips on the Big Issues and Gray Areas of Contemporary American English*.

>> LISA DI MONA

Lark Productions
3 West Main Street, Suite 103
Irvington, NY 10533
Phone: (914) 674-4995; Fax: (914) 674-4387
www.larkproductions.com

I recently received an e-mail query letter that identified the subject/ title and subtitle of the proposed book in the very first sentence, then proceeded in the second paragraph to briefly describe the self-help organization of the book—"explains in 10 steps, etc." I was immediately interested in the subject and its timeliness and the author's get-to-the-point letter had my attention. Her third paragraph let me know who she was and why I should care about her book on this subject related to health and diet. She's a nutritionist at a major university with access to new research. She's also affiliated with a major health club and so has a publicity and promotion vehicle to help sell the book, in addition to her academic credential. Perfect combination of great subject, informed author, and platform.

My only reservation as a busy professional was the fact that she'd sent this letter to many, many agents. Multiple submissions are usually okay by me, but it's better to narrow the scope to a handful of carefully selected representatives.

>> JANE DYSTEL

Dystel & Goderich Literary Management
One Union Square West, Suite 904
New York, NY 10003
(212) 627-9100

It's hard to pick out one query letter from so many over the years. In fact, successful query letters tend to follow the same pattern: well written, focused, friendly but not overly chummy, informative, and descriptive.

One of my novelists, Tayari Jones, impressed me with her very direct approach. She was recommended by another longtime client, Jewell Parker Rhodes, and had had a less than happy experience with another agent prior to contacting me. Her letter told me what she wanted, what her expectations were, and described her novel, *Leaving Atlanta* (about the 1979 murders in that city), in very succinct but enticing terms. She also included relevant newspaper clips that related to the subject of the book and mentioned another then-current title that touched on the same issues. In short, Tayari did her homework and, in a no-nonsense, smart, and eloquent way, made her case for having me represent her. I sold her book and her second novel is about to be published. Those are the kinds of queries I relish.

>> *BARBARA ELLIS*
Scribes Editorial & Literary Agency
318 West 51 Street, Suite 404
New York, NY 10019
Phone: (212) 399-9070; Fax: (212) 242-6513
www.publishersmarketplace.com/members/Scribes/

Just before the holiday season, I received a query letter for a proposal called *The Dog Diet* (*www.thedogdiet.com*), by Patti Lawson (which we're just now shopping), that captured my heart. I was up to my eyeballs in manuscripts and queries when this writer's letter came in, but the title was stimulating and the query sizzled, motivating me to promptly request the proposal. And the proposal delivered everything the query letter promised.

So what was it, first, about the query letter (an author or writer's calling card) that grabbed me and made me so hugely enthusiastic about this title? First, she had an excellent lead. Rather than try to convince me—as so many new writers do—in the first paragraph, about the book's potential, she stated her idea—what the book or proposal was about—and she showed that she understood her idea thoroughly.

Second, the pitch was strong but not overly dramatic or contrived. And while her book was obviously a labor of love, her query demonstrated that she understood that her book was a product. Her letter also showed her as a true professional, and as a writer with the ability and determination to succeed. Finally, she didn't waste words describing material that she had sent along with the query letter, nor did she get carried away with sending too much supporting material. And, at the close of the letter, she confidently asked for the sale.

As to the proposal itself, while we ended up needing to do a bit of reorganization and tightening up, it was clear she had done her homework to the ninth, and had put in the time and effort to perfect her proposal. In the overview it was evident she had a very clear idea of her audience and gave a sharp, concise overview of her concept that beautifully set the stage for what was to follow. The competitive titles section, which included a brief two- or three-line narrative for each title, told me she had a comprehensive understanding of the market and other titles on the bookstore shelves, and where and how her book would fit in. She did not treat the competition cavalierly.

The marketing section was demographically sophisticated from a commercial perspective. The writer also has a very strong platform for writing her book (she does a great deal of speaking, running workshops, writing a column, etc., on her subject, plus she has a lot of media experience and contacts), so the promotion section was an integral part of this particular proposal. It did what any good promotion section should: guide an agent and publisher toward seeing creative and realistic ways to publicize and promote the book, including detailing subsidiary and ancillary potentials for the project. The chapter outlines—the meat of a proposal—were clearly abstracted, and the couple of sample chapters were well developed and showed that the writer could actually pull it off and write the book.

Finally, understanding that the publishing industry is an image-driven business, the proposal was well-packaged: (1) it followed all the general and basic guidelines for submitting a proposal, (2) it was fresh and new (no dog-eared or smudged pages) and carefully and creatively arranged, and (3) again, appreciating the impact of aesthetics, she included a professional and media-savvy picture of her and her dog.

>> *GRACE FREEDSON*
The Publishing Network
E-mail: *gfreedson@worldnet.att.net*

One of the most memorable proposals I received was for a cookbook for creating children's parties. It arrived in an enormous box and contained samples of all the recipes included in the first chapter, all absolutely delicious and a visual delight as well. Sample invitations and party favors were also included. We were really bowled over by the time and effort this author gave to her proposal, and it translated into the same sort of creativity when she was preparing her manuscript.

>> *GEORGE GREENFIELD*
CreativeWell, Inc.
P.O. Box 3130
Memorial Station
Upper Montclair, NJ 07043
Phone: (973) 783-7575; Fax: (973) 783-7530
E-mail: *george@creativewell.com*
www.creativewell.com

I look for book projects that capture my spirit with substance, relevance, and my belief that they deserve to be published. I also consider the lecture potential for the prospective client, as we are both a literary and a lecture agency. There are few professional moments to compare with the discovery of a project that meets all of these criteria and has not yet been seen by anyone else in the publishing community. One such instance came while I was having lunch with Bobby Muller, founder and president of the Vietnam Veterans of America Foundation (VVAF) and cofounder of the Nobel Peace Prize–winning International Campaign to Ban Landmines. I have worked with Bobby since 1980, when I represented him for lectures on Vietnam. Our lecture division was now representing the Campaign for a Landmine Free World, a project of the VVAF. Also attending the lunch was Loung Ung, spokesperson for the Landmines campaign. Loung, a child survivor of the Cambodian genocide, told me that she had written over a hundred pages on her survival when she was sixteen but had never shared them with anyone but the teacher who had encouraged her to write. She agreed to let me see it.

As soon as I read her pages, I knew this was an important book. After months of revisions and development of the proposal, I was ready to submit the project. Yet, the road to publication was surprisingly challenged. Publisher responses ranged from not liking the writing to questioning who would want to read about the Cambodian genocide. With twenty-five submissions and twenty-four rejections, the book was finally sold to HarperCollins. It was bought by Trena Keating, a wonderful senior editor who subsequently became editor-in-chief of Plume. She shared my vision for the project. As they say, "It only takes one." The media upon publication of *First They Killed My Father, A Daughter of Cambodia Remembers* by Loung Ung included a cover story in *USA Today*. On the July Fourth following publication, she was featured on *Nightline*. It didn't stop there. The book won several literary awards, including the 2001 Asian Pacific American Award for Literature (APAAL). I sold translation and publication rights in eleven countries. Loung has now lectured in over eighty communities in the United States and regularly receives standing ovations. She has also been a featured speaker at human rights and other conferences both here and abroad. *First They Killed My Father* has been selected for all-campus and community reads, including those sponsored by American University, University of Iowa, and the state of Vermont, and is required reading in many high school and college courses.

When you have absolute belief in a project, you must sometimes walk through walls of cool rejection before you feel the warm glow of success.

>> ELAINE KOSTER

Elaine Koster Literary Agency, LLC
55 Central Park West, Suite #6
New York, NY 10023
Phone: (212) 362-9488; Fax: (212) 712-0164
E-mail: *elainekost@aol.com*

What always draws my attention in queries, is either previous publishing credits—be they books or stories—and awards and prizes won.

>> SHARLENE MARTIN

Martin Literary Management
17328 Ventura Blvd., Suite 138
Encino (LA), CA 91316
Phone: (818) 595-1130; Fax: (818) 715-0418
www.MartinLiteraryManagement.com

Sharlene Martin sent us the following query letter, which she calls "the worst query letter in the world."

Attn: Martin Literary Management,

I am putting the final touches on my book titled "_____." This is the first book I have ever written. I hope it will be my last book. What I am finding out it is more difficult to get people to read my book than it was for me to write it. I am targeting anybody who enjoys reading a provocative and thought provoking book on life in the United States.

   I have always wanted to write a book but I felt I never had a platform to initiate a book. After being unemployed for nearly 3 years I felt this was the platform for me to start a book. I have critically reflected over my life experiences in the United States. A book on the reflections of life's experiences is nothing new in the literary world. What makes my book different

continued

---

continued

from the others is that I am just a "regular guy" just trying to make sense of the world around me. As a rule books of this type are written by scholars, media celebrities, and politicians but never by John Q. Public.

I would like very much if you would take the time to read this provocative book. I do not expect to make a lot of money on this book. I do realize by not being a professional writer that my sentence structure may not be the best. I feel certain that if my book can be polished up a bit your company stands to make a lot of money.

Sincerely Yours,

>> *ERIN REEL*

The Erin Reel Literary Agency
9006 Wilshire Blvd., Box One
Beverly Hills, CA 90211
(818) 706-3313
E-mail: *erlaquery@sbcglobal.net*

One long-shot query really stands out in my mind, because the author was trying to jump into an already well-established nonfiction parenting market and had virtually no platform. From a market standpoint it was nonstarter; however, the author clearly had talent, personality, and professionalism. Her product caught my interest because she had something to sell. Ultimately, good queries focus on the product.

As I often do with promising but unpublished writers, I offered a few suggestions as to ways to build the strength of her product. In this case the lack of platform was the major obstacle. The book was a commonsense approach to parenting twins by a mother who had done it. Her voice was confident, entertaining, and informative. I suggested she begin by building an interactive Web site and attempt to place articles in mainstream parenting publications. Not only did she take my advice, she pushed hard to accomplish and improve on my suggestions. The willingness to take advice and demonstrate a commitment to the work is always impressive to agents and editors.

After several months of hard work, her platform became quantifiable and several stories on celebrity mothers of twins appeared in a wide range of media outlets. At that point we sent her proposal out to a carefully considered target list and made a sale.

I think most agents and editors will agree, no matter how good a query may be, if it's not on the page, the process ends abruptly. Secondly, if the author isn't friendly and professional, the process ends abruptly. Thirdly, if the author isn't willing to do what it takes to get his or her work published, you've got it, the process ends. No matter how cute and inventive you may be with your query, you must have something to sell.

❯❯ *JODY REIN*
Jody Rein Books, Inc.
www.jodyreinbooks.com

One query letter I answered with a phone call five minutes after I read it was the pitch for *The Big Year* by Mark Obmascik (Free Press, 2004). Here's why:

(1) *The idea:* A nonfiction book tracking three obsessed birdwatchers—was absolutely original and fresh.
(2) *The concept fit my agency perfectly:* I love quirky narrative nonfiction, on topics that have an established audience.
(3) *I was already a fan of the author.* I knew his great work as a newspaper columnist, and respected him.
(4) *The author's fields of expertise.* Journalism AND the environment—matched his topic and
(5) *A great letter.* The letter was well written and fun to read.

It seemed a natural hit to me. And it was. The proposal sold to Simon & Schuster after a hotly contested, big-money auction, and the book went on to be a *New York Times* bestseller, *Entertainment Weekly* "Editors' Choice," a BookSense pick, a Barnes and Noble Discover New Writers pick, a *Sports Illustrated* four-page serial, and has been optioned by DreamWorks for a movie.

❯❯ CAROL SUSAN ROTH

Carol Susan Roth Literary
1824 Oak Creek Drive, Suite #416
Palo Alto, CA 94304
E-mail: *carol@authorsbest.com*

At the peak of the dot-com boom, I received a FedEx from a fellow associated with one of the country's largest investment newsletter companies. I saw his letterhead and my heart started beating like a drum!

He indicated that his company would commit six figures to the promotion and had financial resources, the media, and online contacts to back it. Many authors promise to do all sorts of promotion for their book but I knew that he could and would!

This expert only had a title—not even a proposal. I immediately phoned him and he happened to be in SF visiting. We had lunch the next day and he signed on as my client.

I found him a writer and a publisher and within six months we had a *New York Times, Wall Street Journal,* and *USA Today* bestseller!!

❯❯ JAMES SCHIAVONE

Schiavone Literary Agency, Inc.
236 Trails End
West Palm Beach, FL 33413-2135
Phone/fax: (561) 966-9294

NY Branch Office (June, July, August, only)
3671 Hudson Manor Terrace, #11H
Bronx, NY 10463-1139
Phone/fax: (718) 548-5332

Among the hundred-plus queries I receive each week, I must uncover those that are engaging and marketable. An initial query letter from

Michael G. Santos, an inmate at a minimum-security federal camp in Colorado, immediately piqued my interest, based on his continuous accomplishments under incarceration. He earned a bachelor's degree from Mercer and an M.A. degree from Hofstra. The college degrees, coupled with three books published by prestigious academic presses, deserved my attention. His publications were much too academic for the general-interest reader. Given the astounding and growing number of American prison inmates, I believed that I could sell a straightforward nonacademic account of living in prison that would inform the reading public about conditions in American prisons.

I am a firm believer in the importance of a well-executed, professional proposal for nonfiction works. The days of editors like Maxwell Perkins, who were able to publish their authors of choice, no longer exist. An editor, no matter how enamored he or she may be about an author's work, can no longer make a unilateral decision to publish a book. Instead, he or she must face his or her associates in a "pub" meeting and convince them of the viability and marketability of the book. Often the sales department can put the kibosh on a project they do not believe they can sell. Therefore, the author must provide the editor with as much ammunition as possible. By presenting the concept, competition, marketing strategies, etc., along with at least two or three sample chapters, the author provides the impetus for agreement among the editorial staff.

I suggested to Michael that he check out books on publishing that guide readers in the preparation of a book proposal. Often, solid outlines and ideas are suggested and when followed result in the development of a winning proposal. Michael followed up and sent me a great proposal for his book, *Living in Prison: The Vicious Circle.* Within ten days of making multiple submissions, I received a call from an editor at St. Martin's Press expressing interest in the work. A contract was negotiated and St. Martin's will publish the book in 2006 or perhaps sooner.

My advice to authors is always query first. Then if you are asked to send a proposal, do some homework and get that winning proposal off to the agent.

❯❯ BOB SILVERSTEIN

Quicksilver Books
Literary Agents
508 Central Park Avenue, #5101
Scarsdale, NY 10583
E-mail: *quickbooks@optonline.net*
www.quicksilverbooks.com

First, let me tell you about query letters that immediately turn me off:

- When they are typed on an old typewriter or, worse, handwritten and often illegible. The graphic look of a query letter is important in making a good first impression. Use a computer!
- Those that list multiple projects and crossover genres; for example, novel #1 is Sci-fi, novel #2 is a Western, novel #3 is a Young Adult, et cetera. This kind of shotgun approach is bound to backfire.
- Ones that make no mention of an author's credentials. Story line is important but so is the writer's provenance. Establish your qualifications for writing about the subject.
- Letters that do not address me specifically, but are written to "Dear Agent" or "To Whom It May Concern." I think it's important that an author make an effort to find out the agent's name and to know what the agency is looking for in terms of categories, whether fiction or nonfiction.
- And finally, letters that go on for three pages or more. As far as I'm concerned, one page—two at most—should be sufficient.

OK, so much for the negative . . . now to the positive.

For me, the best and most effective query letters do the following:

1. They immediately establish the author as someone to take seriously; for example:
   a. "I'm a member of the National Writers Union."

b. "My name is such and such and I'm the author of a book (or books) previously published by Little, Brown (or some other mainstream house)."

c. "You were recommended to me by so-and-so (one of our clients or at least a person of reputation)."

2. They include reviews, news clips, flyers, etc., that showcase the author as a person with a platform, media exposure, and marketing capability. This may not be as important for fiction, but it is especially crucial in many nonfiction categories that an author have credentials and endorsements from peers, celebrities, etc. Just as agents have to sell a project to publishers, likewise authors must sell themselves to agents. So always put your best foot forward when you make your pitch! And keep in mind the adage, "Publishers print, authors sell!"

Here's an example of a query letter that immediately grabbed my attention and eventually landed me a client, bestselling author and friend all at the same time:

Dear Mr. Silverstein:

As an author, psychologist, and executive coach, I've spent the past 25 years helping people get—and keep—the jobs they want. My last book _____ was named "the best unsung business book of the year" by *Fast Company* magazine. I'm writing to ask that Quicksilver Books consider representing my next work, _____.

From there the letter goes on to describe the book in two succinct paragraphs. Then comes the all-important marketing information:

In addition to my several well-received books related to women's issues, I've also had numerous articles published in professional journals

continued

continued

and been interviewed for television, magazines, and newspapers. I am committed to being a full participant in the process required to ensure the success of _____. It would be a pleasure to send you the full proposal and press kit. I look forward to hearing from you and thank you in advance for your time and consideration.

Sincerely,

Author's name

The letter was written on the author's letterhead, and that in itself was a plus.

Fiction queries usually take a slightly different form, but the end result is the same: Make it succinct, exciting, intelligent, and inviting.

CHAPTER
9

"Some books are undeservedly forgotten; none are undeservedly remembered."
W. H. Auden

Finding the Best Agent for You

THIS CHAPTER WILL COVER:

▶ Clarify what you want
▶ Be proactive
▶ Track record
▶ Interview checklist
▶ Face-to-face meetings
▶ Questions to ask
▶ Check sources

NOW THAT YOU KNOW the sources you can tap to gather information about agents and the steps to take to increase your appeal, zero in on identifying those agents who could be best for you.

Frequently, when authors start the process of looking for agents, they take a limited or defeatist approach. They assume that since agents are selective in taking new clients, they won't have many options. So they sign up with the first agent who shows interest, which can turn into a disaster.

If, as we suggested, you develop a solid plan and conduct the necessary research to learn about and find agents, you should be in a position to have choices. Don't start your search by looking for the perfect agent; start instead by making a list of those who could work. Pull a group of names together and then systematically proceed from there.

It's to your advantage to create a pool of potential agents and then to sift through that group. In the process, you will learn about agents

Rick Says

"Shop around for an agent! The process of finding the right agent may not be as one-sided as you've been led to believe. Agents need writers as much as writers need agents. Without new clients, agents can't survive; new clients are agents' life-blood. So agents are always open to signing new talent.

"The bottom line is that if you do your homework, are fully prepared, and have what it takes, agents will be eager to represent you."

and gain more experience and comfort in dealing with them. You will find out, firsthand, what they think, how they work, and what they want. Then, if any of your choices rejects you, you will still have others you can approach. Plus, you will learn what changes you should make to improve your submissions and you won't be as likely to become discouraged.

Clarify What You Want

Begin your search for the right agent as if it were a campaign; plan it carefully and don't leave it to chance. Decide on the direction you intend to take and then map out the steps to get there. Examine your strengths and weaknesses and try to find an agent who can best fill in your gaps. For example, you may need an agent who can help you with your writing skills, business skills, platform development, or career planning.

If you encounter resistance along the way, don't quit or abdicate control. Be persistent and remain in charge. Don't let agents bully you or even imply that they are doing you a favor by considering you as a client. Similarly, don't take a high-handed or overly aggressive stance with them. Agents avoid potential clients who think that they're the best things that ever happened to publishing. Remember when you search for the right agent that you are seeking a business partner, someone with whom you can work productively for years. Think in terms of your career, not just this one book.

Most agents are thinking about the long term as well. They don't just want literary one-night stands; they want authors who are going to turn out books on a regular basis. Agent Michael Larsen says agents want clients with "Nichecraft," ideas that can become series of books that authors will enjoy writing and promoting and that can launch their careers. "Each new book in the series becomes its own profit center. In a series, a synergy is created and all the books in the series help sell each other," Larsen notes.

Before you jump in, clarify exactly what you want from an agent. Take time to think about it fully and make a list of exactly the specific items you want. Identify precisely what you would like from an agency and prioritize the items on your list.

Some of your objectives could be an agent who will:

- Just sell this one book.
- Sell this book and its film rights.
- Build, chart and manage your writing career.
- Know the market for your type of book or books. Perhaps you're a nonfiction writer, but you also want to write a memoir or a fictional children's book. See if particular agents can serve your varied goals.
- Be your literary and/or business advisor.
- Be your confidant.
- Be your mentor, teacher, or guide.
- All of the above.

Knowing clearly what you want will make it easier for you to focus your search. It will help you eliminate some candidates and make others stand out.

Although it's crucial to know precisely what you want of an agent, it's equally important to remain open to the input an agent can provide. As publishing experts, agents can bring great and unexpected value to your relationship. They can contribute insights and ideas that probably never would have occurred to you. They can bring contacts and connections that can expand your reach, move you into new, uncharted areas, and dramatically change the direction and scope of your career.

Be Proactive

Writers are always being edited. After a while, they get used to it and tend to accept what others say. Writers are accustomed to dealing with people who voice strong opinions on what writers should say and how they should say it. Agents are no exception.

When someone receives so much editing, his or her strength can be lost; feelings that fuel a writer's writing can be diminished or quenched, usually for commercial or practical reasons. In the face of obstacles—and you will encounter many—it's up to you to keep your fire aflame.

Some agents may try to move you in directions that don't feel right. Frequently, they want you to move your writing in a more commercial vein or simplify it to reach broader audiences. Although following their advice can make the difference between whether you get published or not, it may not move you toward your long-term career goals.

When it comes to your writing and your career, always take the position that you are the expert, the boss, and the final authority. You must have veto power because no one knows or cares as much about your writing as you; no one has as much at stake. You must:

- Make or agree with all major decisions your agent makes.
- Maintain the right to approve all final decisions that cost more than a stated amount.
- Receive periodic updates.
- Be able to speak with your agent when you need him or her.

Updates will inform you whether your project is proceeding on schedule, what problems occurred, and what changes you could make. Regular updates will also help you make quick adjustments to address problems.

Don't discount your values. Look for an agent you will feel proud, not ashamed, to be associated with. A few dishonest and disreputable individuals have infiltrated the literary agency business and they can be charming and convincing. If you have misgivings, trust your instincts and walk away no matter how badly you want to be published. Your agent will be your spokesperson and your representative. People will judge you by those with whom you associate.

Look for an agent who will shape your career in directions that are consistent with your values and what you want in your life. Identify the values that are most important to you and what you want so you can make choices that are consistent with them. It's always easier, and usually more successful, to work with people who share your values.

An agent needs to be someone you can trust. For an author/agent relationship to work well, you will need to:

- Not interfere, prevent, or make it more difficult for your agent to do his or her job. Being overly involved could be counter-productive, breed resentment, and cause your project to suffer. People generally resent being micromanaged.
- Leave the details to the professionals. Assume the role of a resource who is willing to make changes that will enhance your agent's performance; to make it easier or more productive.

Show That You Are Serious

To find an agent and prove to him or her that you and your book idea are worth representing, you may have to get creative and take some active steps. For example, consider attending BookExpo, the huge annual tradeshow attended by people and companies in book publishing. Harriette Bawarsky wanted to write a book on Alzheimer's disease, which afflicted her mother. When she began to research potential publishers online, she quickly realized that she had to become an advocate for her book.

Through her research, Harriette learned about BookExpo, and so she decided to go. To prepare, Harriette checked the online booksellers to learn which houses published books on Alzheimer's disease. She then created a list of potential publishers for her book and checked the BookExpo Web site to see which of them would be at the tradeshow. Harried pared her list to those publishers she wanted to meet and set out to accomplish her goal.

Traditionally, most publishers don't go to BookExpo primarily to find new authors. They're usually more concerned with promoting their lists than with finding new works. Nevertheless, many tenacious writers attend BookExpo to network, and some bring proposals. Harriette prepared a one-page synopsis of her book and delivered it to the publishers on her list and gave them her short, well-practiced pitch.

When Harriette received positive responses from editors, she took their business cards and wrote down their comments. Then she took her list of interested publishers and the names of the encouraging editors to a literary agent, whom she convinced that her book idea was viable. Harriette signed with the agent and her project is now moving forward.

Track Record

Although those who consider themselves literary managers might disagree, the fundamental service that agents provide is selling their clients' books. The primary reason writers go to agents is to get their books sold. So, always obtain information on prospective agents' sales histories.

Ask for a list of the agent's sales for the past several years. The agent should be willing, even proud, to comply. The good ones can, and frequently will, rattle the names right off for you. They will have up-to-date sales information posted on their Web sites and printouts on hand.

If an agent resists giving you the titles of the books he or she recently sold or insists that such information is confidential, watch out. Most agents aren't bashful about their sales and something will probably be amiss; most likely, it's lack of sales or client problems.

When you get the list,

- Note the types of books the agent sold and those that are similar to your book. It's advantageous to have an agent who knows your book's genre and has made sales in it.
- Verify the sales by checking with online booksellers and on the listed publishers' sites. Agents have been known to be creative with their sales information.
- Research publishers. Thousands of companies publish books, so check that the names on the agent's list actually exist, if they published other books, and how solid they seem.

If you are considering hiring a person who recently became an agent, make sure he or she has a solid publishing background with at least a few years in the business. Experience dealing with books of your genre would be an added bonus.

Industry outsiders, even experienced publishing attorneys, may take a while in the business to get up to speed. Contacts and an understanding of the publishing industry are essential to an agent. So don't even think of using anyone who doesn't have a publishing background, because they will learn on your dime and probably won't do the best job.

Interview Checklist

When you are trying to find an agent, you have every right to question and interview them. Unfortunately, most writers don't interview agents and simply sign with whoever agrees to represent them. While agents are qualifying you as a prospective client, qualify them as potential agents. When interviewing with an agent:

- Keep a balance. Answer their questions, but also listen.
- Don't dominate the conversation and put all your focus on selling yourself. Agents will be looking for specific answers from

you and if you don't let them ask them, they may decide not to represent you.

- After you respond to agents' inquiries, question them. Get answers and obtain information so that you can make the best possible decision.
- Don't be pushy, but be direct and say what's on your mind. Remember that you will be entering into a business relationship that could involve a lot of money.

Some agents may act dismissively. They know they're in demand and that writers are in great supply. They may try to make you feel that you're lucky that they're giving you their precious time.

Despite how badly you may want an agent, factor this kind of attitude into your decision. Seriously consider whether you want to work with, be represented by, and put money in the pocket of someone who seems to look down on you.

Questions to Ask

The questions that you should ask prospective agents will vary project to project. However, the following basic questions are appropriate in most situations. Also use these to generate additional, more focused, questions. They are:

- Do you specialize in a particular genre of books?
- What have you recently sold that you are most excited about?
- I noticed that you sold X; how did that author get your attention?
- May I have a list of your current and past clients?
- May I contact your clients?
- May I have a list of the books you sold in the past year?
- What books that are similar to mine have you sold?
- Are you a member of AAR?
- Will you adhere to the AAR Canon of Ethics?
  - If not, please explain.

- How much should I expect my book to sell for to a publisher?
- Who will lead my account?
- What is his/her experience?
- How much time will he/she spend on my account?
- Who else will work on my account?
  - In what capacity?
  - What is his/her experience?
  - How much time will he/she devote to my account?
- Who will supervise the work on my account?
  - What is his/her experience?
  - How much time will he/she put in on my account?
- What is your plan for selling my book?
- How long do you expect it to take?
- What more can I do to increase my book's chances of selling?
- How much input will I have in my campaign?
- How often will I receive communications about my account?
- How often will I get updates on my account?
- In addition to selling my book, what services will I receive?
  - In what time frame will I receive each of these services?
- What can I do if I don't receive the results promised?
  - Can I fire you?
  - If so, when?
  - Will you still be entitled to fee payments?
  - If so,
    - For what and
    - How much?
- What are your strong points, your advantages over other agencies?
- What is the best way and best time for me to contact you?
- How long should I expect to wait before hearing from you?
- Do you have a protocol for how we will work together?
  - If so, what is it?
- Do you have an author/agent agreement?
  - If so, may I see it?

"You want an agent who will be totally honest with you," agent John Willig stresses. "You have to have the skin to hear the hard truth and act on it. Usually, writers hear from their friends and their immediate world how great their book is. First, before they go to an agent, they should go to writing professionals, who can tell them the truth about what they have to do to write a quality book. Agents don't have the time to do that so it makes sense to do it before you go to an agent."

Check Sources

Getting references can be a waste of time because most people will give you the names of only those people who will speak glowingly about them. To avoid this problem, don't ask agents which clients you can contact. Instead, ask for their entire client list and contact whomever you wish. If an agent won't give you permission to contact his or her clients, consider moving on. When you contact an agent's clients, the following are some of the questions you should ask:

- On a scale of 1 to 10, 10 being the highest, how would you rate:
  - Your agent's representation of you?
  - Your agent's results in selling your book?
  - The quality of your agent's advice?
  - The overall experience of working with your agent?
- What about your agent do you especially like?
- What about your agent do you not like?
- What could your agent do better?
- Does your agent always take your calls and e-mails?
- How long does it usually take?
- Does your agent give clear, responsive answers to your questions?
- Does your agent truly understand your work, goals, and values?
- Does your agent welcome your input?
- Do you have any questions about your agent's charges?
  - If so, what are they?

- How long does it take for you to receive royalty statements and checks?
- Is your agent pleasant and supportive to work with?
- What irritates, annoys, or angers your agent?
- Will your agent stand up and fight for you with the editor and/or publisher?
- Is your agent creative?
- Is your agent persistent?
- Is your agent honest?
- Is your agent fair?
- Does your agent frequently seek opportunities to advance your career?
- Would you hire your agent again?
- Who else would you suggest that I contact?

Face-to-Face Meetings

Before you sign on, try to meet all the candidates to become your agent. Spend time with them. Get a sense of who they are, how well you might work together and what the chemistry or relationship could be. Sometimes you know right away that this is the perfect match, and on other occasions you instinctively know that it won't work.

"Over the years, when my agent gives my name as a referral, it has been my pleasure to recommend her highly. If an agent is eager to sign you, request permission to speak to a few of his or her clients. Why not? You may be about to put your writing career in the hands of this agent and it can be extremely helpful to get some perspective from someone he or she represents."

Ask yourself if you would want these individuals to represent you, advise you, shape your career, and champion your books to editors and publishers. Do you feel that you can trust them?

Agents may not want to meet you before you sign with them. Since agents reject more than 90 percent of the submissions they receive, it doesn't make sense for them to meet writers until they are confident that they will work together.

If agents resist, don't give up easily. Make it clear that your meeting doesn't have to be long and elaborate, but stress that it's important for you to meet. If an agent has a good feeling about you and your work, he or she will make the time for you to meet.

Whenever possible, set up a lunch meeting with a prospective agent. This is a good way to get to know him or her. Don't just try to sell your book idea, but approach it as an informational meeting. Learn about his or her pet peeves, interests, and points of view. Talk about the special qualities of the books he or she sold recently.

Let the agent select the restaurant so it's convenient to his or her office and doesn't take too much of his or her time. Be generous and pick up the check; it's deductible and can mean a lot to agents because they usually are expected to grab the check.

An author we know flew to New York just to interview three agents. Initially, they reluctantly consented to spend ten minutes with her. Each of those ten-minute meetings turned into one-and-a-half-hour lunches. During one lunch, the agent really spiked her interest; they hit it off personally and shared common perspectives, goals, and values. The agent immediately grasped her book idea and suggested a terrific new slant, and she felt assured that he would represent her passionately. What our friend accomplished during that lunch meeting would not have been possible had they not met and spent time together.

Action Steps

1. List exactly what you would like an agent to provide for you and prioritize your list.
2. Give three examples of how you can be proactive in finding and working with an agent.
3. What steps should you take when you get a list of a prospective agent's sales?
4. Customize a list of questions to ask prospective agents.
5. Explain the value of meeting face-to-face with prospective agents.

Remember:

 Compile a list of potential agents. Examine your strengths and weaknesses and try to find an agent who can best fill in your gaps. Look for an agent who you would trust to be your business partner, someone with whom you could work productively for years.

 Check prospective agents' Web sites and ask for a list of their sales for the past several years. Review and ask the questions on the interview checklist; contact the people the agent gives as references. Try to meet all prospective agents face-to-face before you sign. Then, review how you should proceed to interest the right agent in you.

CHAPTER 10

"The secret to creativity is knowing how to hide your sources."
Albert Einstein

How to Interest the Right Agent

THIS CHAPTER WILL COVER:

▶ Conduct research
▶ Values
▶ Meet face-to-face
▶ Attend conferences
▶ Go with your strengths
▶ New agents

ATTRACTING THE INTEREST of the right agent can be as mystifying and elusive as interesting the man or woman of your dreams. How to do it depends on many factors, including chemistry, timing, luck, and so many unknowns that we wouldn't be foolish enough to try to list them.

How to interest the right agent is a question without one correct answer; lots of approaches may work, but not in every situation. Unfortunately, we must confess, we don't know of one guaranteed, absolute, can't-miss sure thing, but we do have a few suggestions that you should bear in mind.

Excuse us for being repetitive, but the best way to interest the right agent is to start by going through all of the steps that we've laid out in this book. Gather information about the agents and find out all you can about them, but this time concentrate on looking for qualities or values that you may share, which could make a particular agent the ideal representative for you.

So check the guidebooks, online guides, and agents' Web sites. Examine other books written in styles, approaches, or formats like yours as well as titles that you really admire. Also see what others have said about agents on Google groups(*http://groups.google.com*), Editors & Preditors *(www.anotherealm.com/prededitors)*, Science Fiction Writer's Association's Writer Beware (*www.sfwa.org/beware/agents.html*), and other sources. Network with other writers to get their insights and recommendations.

In your research, look for links shared by you and an agent. One of the best connections may be the authors and titles the agent represents. If an agent found and represents an author and a book that you really love or identify strongly with, you may have similar tastes, feelings, ideas, or values. Agents who sold those books may be more likely to understand you, your writing, and what you need to say.

Often, the agents who will intrigue you the most will also find you and your project interesting. Trust your instincts; often links or connections can be based on reasons that we can't identify or articulate, but we just feel that they exist. So if you find yourself liking or being drawn to a particular agent, trust your feelings.

Learn All You Can

Make it your mission to learn lots about agents because the more information you collect, the better your chances of making the right choice. Gathering information will also help you to make a great impression on agents by showing them how serious and professional you are.

Agents may also be flattered that you made a strong effort to learn about them. They know that writers have many options and may be pleased that you elected to target them.

"Before you contact any agent, go to his or her Web site and look at his or her past sales," Encino, California, agent Sharlene Martin suggests. "See if they've done books on or close to your topic. Check the books they are currently offering and you'll see a consistency in the type of books they're responding to."

The first thing Martin loves to see is that writers have researched her, that they've been to her Web site and know something about her. "When a letter starts, 'Congratulations on your recent sale of _____ ,' or 'What a wonderful testimonial for you your client so-and-so wrote,' it makes me feel that they are targeting their query on me," Martin states.

Values

One of the most essential ingredients in forging strong relationships is having shared values. Values are what you prize and esteem, the beliefs that are most important to you, and what you want most in life. Your values may be to search for truth, to build world peace, to make money, to have a great time, or to continually learn.

When people share common values, they bond; a link connects them and makes them partners, teammates, and comrades at arms. Shared values make the work they do together take on a higher meaning; it helps them achieve together what neither of them might accomplish alone.

Identify your values; clarify for yourself what you most deeply believe and what you really want. Since your book is probably aligned with your values, look for an agent who will be on the same page.

Finding an agent who shares your values can make the process of being an author more enjoyable, powerful, and successful. In your research, try to get an indication of what each agent believes, from the types of books they sell, the organizations they belong to and the places they appear. Try to determine what they value.

Pay special attention to the entries on agents in Jeff Herman's *Guide to Book Publishers, Editors, & Literary Agents* (The Writer Books). The agents' answers to Herman's questions can be revealing and can give you a sense of the agent and his or her values.

When it comes to assessing your values, be honest with yourself. If your primary objective is to sell your book, concentrate on those agents who can best help you reach that goal.

Meet Face-to-Face

As we recommended in the previous chapter, try to meet agents face-to-face. Little can provide you with as much insight as a direct meeting where you can spend time with and observe people with whom you may work.

When you meet, try to get a sense of who the agent is. Ask yourself the following questions:

- Do you like him or her?
- Do you feel you have anything in common?
- Do you trust him or her?
- Would you follow his or her advice?
- Are you comfortable in his or her presence?
- Do you feel hesitant to speak?
- Would you want this person to:
  - Represent you?
  - Advise you?
  - Guide your career?
  - Champion your books to editors and publishers?

Attend Conferences

Literary agents attend many writers' conferences and one of the reasons they do so is to meet new writers. At these conferences, many authors have connected with agents or leveraged their contacts to find representatives. Information on writers' conferences can be found at Writer's Digest (*www.writersdigest.com*) and ShawGuides (*http://writing.shawguides.com*).

Bonnie Marson, the author of *Sleeping With Schubert* (Random House, 2004), used a writers' conference to find an agent. Here's Bonnie's story in her own words, which she was kind enough to write for us. Thanks, Bonnie.

"Be an Open Book"

Professional writers often prefer to guard their work, sharing it on a need-to-know basis with discretion and good judgment. Not me. I beat the odds with my first book, armed only with my manuscript, a newcomer's enthusiasm, and full disclosure (aka, my big mouth).

I was a lifelong artist and had written only one piece of fiction, a short story, before writing my novel, *Sleeping With Schubert*. I had no experience or plan to help me through the process from manuscript to publication. Staying open helped me in every way.

First of all, since I had no expectations, I was unburdened by any publish-or-die anxiety. I could open up and allow the story to flow without struggle or self-imposed pressure.

On the totally practically side, I was open with people about what I was doing. Not ready to use the words "I'm writing a book" (too daunting by far), I told friends, family, and colleagues that I was working on "my brilliant novel." That made me smile, and they got a kick out of the notion. And because I told people what I was doing, I never had to ask for help; they offered it on their own.

When I was halfway through my manuscript, a friend invited me to a University of New Mexico writers' conference in Taos. I was with a group of experienced writers and aspiring novelists. They were inspiring, encouraging people with a wealth of knowledge that I needed and they happily shared.

With finished manuscript in hand, I bought the highly recommended *Guide to Literary Agents*. Scared myself silly. Thousands of names, and where would I start? Who's really good, and which ones should I approach? Luckily, I had told a friend in Hawaii about my manuscript, and she suggested submitting it through the Maui Writers Conference Manuscript Marketplace at *www.mauiwriters.com/mwc_manuscript.html*. You don't have to attend the conference to use the Manuscript Marketplace, which is a service that gets your query to reputable agents who might be interested in your kind of work.

The Manuscript Marketplace sends you a query format that you follow exactly according to instructions. It may seem restrictive, but the succinctness actually helps. It's your chance to take your work and distill it to its scintillating essence. Give the readers a nice, juicy taste of your story, with examples of your style and appeal. Create a query that's rich, evocative, and leaves them wanting more.

You submit your Marketplace query by a certain date and—here's the good part—you get all the answers on a given date a few months later. (This is a big relief to anyone who's sent queries to agents, then sat hoping and waiting, never knowing if or when a reply might come.) You receive a list of all agents who read your query and those who want to see more of your work. There's a $149 fee for the Marketplace's distribution and administration service, and it's well worth it. I had five interested agents as a result.

Through the Manuscript Marketplace, I found a wonderful agent and was close to signing with her. But me and my big mouth. I told a colleague, Dan Baker—someone I didn't know well at the time—what I was doing. Dan's also an author, and he said to me, "Don't sign with anyone until you talk to my agent, Richard Pine. Best in the business."

I called Richard Pine, we clicked, and he loved the book. After some revisions, he sold it to Random House in one week.

If I hadn't been open about my book all along the way, it would probably be sitting in a desk drawer today. In fact, there are surely great manuscripts all over the world that are hidden away in attics, abandoned by authors who gave up hope.

Your book won't find its way to an agent without you. "The End" finishes your story, but not your work. You owe your book an introduction to the world and a great query that will get it noticed.

Be an open book so your book gets opened.

Go with Your Strengths

If you want the right agent to recognize your strength and talent, you must present yourself in the best light. Assess your strengths as a writer. Ask your friends, colleagues, and other writers to tell you what they like

Robyn Says

"If you have something special, a driving force or powerful message that you passionately want to express, put it out there and someone will hear you. Take action. Too many people just sit silently with their great ideas. Then, when someone else finally does it, they say, 'I thought of that!' But they never acted on their ideas.

"Remember that all agents differ; they have diverse interests, likes, dislikes, tastes, reactions, and standards. All it takes is one to recognize your talent, to be intrigued with you, to understand the importance of your book, and to agree to try to launch your career. Finding a great agent is like winning the lottery."

best about your writing. You may be surprised by what they say. Get a writing professional to critique your work and evaluate your strengths and weaknesses.

When you draft your queries, capitalize on the strengths others have identified. Then look for agents who represent authors with similar strengths. Emphasize your strong points in your submissions to agents. Let them see what you do best; it should bring you better, more positive responses.

Despite the publishing industry's bottom-line focus, the romance hasn't entirely gone out of the business; it has not completely disappeared. Most agents are devoted to books and writing. Despite the constant reading, pressure, long hours, and tough negotiations, they have a deep passion for their work. They're suckers for a great story, they love new ideas, and they're moved by artfully crafted prose. They want to be swept away and to find writing that moves, stimulates, and teaches them and makes them think.

Most of all, agents are awed by great talent, especially when it's new talent. They love the discovery; finding new voices and books. Many agents also live for the uphill battle, championing great talent and proving to all doubters its worth.

Chapter 10 ■ How to Interest the Right Agent

As a result, many agents are willing to take a risk, to represent an author who doesn't fit the mold. They may decide to sign a writer and build his or her platform or shape his or her writing, ideas, or style.

That one individual, the agent who really gets you and your book, can be "the right agent." If such an agent has an affinity for you and your work, he or she may know editors with similar tastes. He or she may know how to package and frame your submissions to create the most interest.

New York City agent June Clark tells us that she will give her all to an author if she's moved by the project in some way, if she says, "Wow, what a great idea. I would love to read that book." When her enthusiasm is there, it gets through to the author, which makes it better for them to work together.

Clark responds to query letters that are earnest, dynamic, and heartfelt or where the author isn't afraid to be a little edgy and vulnerable.

Above all, Berkeley, California, agent Andree Abecassis of the Ann Elmo Agency respects professionalism. She respects people "who (1) write well, who are (2) passionate about their topics and (3) meet their deadlines. It also helps to be honest, but that's a part of being professional; it's a building block for trust."

"I'm always stunned when someone comes along with a quirky idea and I may find two editors that I will try, who are willing to take a chance," she says. "It's still a business of falling in love with an idea. The same thing happens to me as an agent."

Abecassis doesn't take projects that she's not interested in. She will simply tell the prospective client that she doesn't think that she's the right agent for this project. "It's not fair to the author," she explains. "Authors deserve to be represented by agents who wholeheartedly want to represent them. They have to be truly interested in the subject and love the way the writer writes so much that the subject doesn't matter."

When writers contact agents, Abecassis adds, "they should be engaging, pleasant, and hang in there. Writers must persevere."

New Agents

New agents may be inexperienced, but they can be the ideal representatives for new and unpublished writers. They may also have extensive experience because they did virtually everything an agent does when they worked for publishing companies.

Newcomers to the literary agency business usually need clients and frequently will be willing to take risks. They may gamble on authors that established agents reject.

To find new agents, look through the guidebooks, which generally give the year the agency was established or when individuals became agents.

"To build their careers, new agents may work harder, they may go the extra mile and try to be more creative in making sales. New agents often come fresh out of publishing so they still have close industry contacts and know what publishers need. They also may not be as linked to certain editors or publishers or have the conflicts of interest that can compromise more experienced reps."

Action Steps

1. Set forth the values that are most important to you.
2. List five qualities that you would hope to discover in a face-to-face meeting with a prospective agent.
3. What writers' conferences could you attend in the next year?
4. List your strengths as a writer (yes, you can include promotional strength).
5. Could it be advantageous for you to work with a new agent? If so, list why.

Remember:

⚠ Get a sense of agents by networking and checking the guidebooks, online guides, and agents' Web sites. Find out which agents represented books written in styles, approaches, or formats similar to yours as well as titles that you really admire. See what others have said about them in online groups and Web sites. Contact other writers to get their input.

⚠ Look for candidates who share your values and try to meet them. Consider new, less experienced agents. They may have extensive experience working for publishing companies, understand the market, have great contacts, and work harder for you. Also, they may not place such a premium on your lack of a platform.

CHAPTER
11

"With advertising, you pay for it; with publicity you pray for it."
Anonymous

.

Why Agents Love Platforms

THIS CHAPTER WILL COVER:

► Publishers' requirements
► Building a platform
► Platform alternatives

FOR NONFICTION WRITERS, the most significant development of the past decade has been the insistence by publishers that authors have national platforms. For fiction writers, authors' platforms matter less. However, it never hurts for a fiction writer to be charismatic, articulate, a vigorous promoter, and media savvy.

Children's book writers and illustrators also benefit from being willing to travel, visit bookstores, network, and promote. While authors have succeeded without having great public personas or large followings who buy their books, today's nonfiction writers need every possible advantage to attract agents who will go to war for them.

Agents gravitate to writers with visibility and reach because they're the type of authors publishers want. Publishers are convinced that authors who have national platforms generate more book sales, so literary agents look for clients who have platforms because they are the authors they can sell.

For authors of business, psychology, parenting, and relationship books, a national platform is now almost mandatory. Although exceptions do exist, agents generally won't represent authors who don't regularly speak publicly, teach, write articles or columns, and have a strong media and Internet presence and professional affiliations.

Agents make more money selling books to large publishers because the big guys pay more. Since the large publishers are now insisting on authors with national platforms, agents are following suit. Occasionally, some agents will roll the dice with an author who doesn't have a platform. For example, if New York City agent Liv Bloomer finds authors who have something special, she says, "I'll take them, but I can't have too many of them at one time."

"It's a crowded marketplace," agent John Willig, president and founder of Literary Services, Inc., explains. "So publishers are looking for writers who write books that are aligned with the author's everyday work and practice. That alignment today is critical, plus the author must be involved in activities that can support the sales of the book's message, like speeches, workshops, and e-mail communities."

"It's not enough to just have the great idea or to have that great idea and be a great writer. Today, you also have to have a platform, which is a word taken from the IT world," Willig notes. "A platform translates to publishers as energy behind the book; it tells them that the author, the author's company, the author's e-mail community, and the author's following will help move the book in an extremely crowded marketplace."

Exceptions

Some exceptions do exist, Berkeley, California, agent Andree Abecassis says. "The market is media driven, it's celebrity driven—unfortunate, but true. The ideal nonfiction writer must have contacts in his or her field and promote whatever the project is or it's almost impossible to sell to a major, commercial house."

"However, it always comes down to the idea," Abecassis continues. "If a writer has a good idea and no platform, but I really liked the idea, I might try. After all, there must have been a point when nobody knew Suze Orman."

"I'm always stunned when someone comes along with a quirky idea, and I may find one or two editors who are willing to take a chance. It's still a business of falling in love with an idea," which Abecassis admits also happens to her as an agent.

Publishers want authors with platforms because it's hard for books to become top sellers without authors' platforms. As the insiders say, they can't "break them out." According to publishing guru Michael Larsen, a San Francisco agent and the author of *Literary Agents: What They Do, How They Do It, and How to Find and Work with the Right One for You* (John Wiley & Sons, 1996), "A platform is vital if an author: (a) wants to be published by a big house, and (b) the book is the type that requires author promotion. If an author has enough promotional ammunition, the author or his or her agent can approach big houses right away."

"Say you're a woman who spent her entire life raising kids, owned a very successful day-care center or was a foster mom, who had successfully raised many children, her own and those she took," June Clark, a New York City agent, says. "If she wanted to write a parenting book, they would look at her and say, 'You don't have a platform.' It wasn't like that years ago. Now, you have to be a nurse, a pediatrician, a child psychologist, and have a following. A couple of people have snuck under that wire who were witty writers or journalists with contacts, but it's very, very difficult," Clark declares.

The platform requirement has filtered through the publishing world. Second- and third-tier publishers and even small, specialty houses are now demanding platforms. The requirement is not only entrenched, but the level of the platform is continually being raised.

Roger Cooper, executive vice president of I Books, Inc., observes, "The level of the platform keeps increasing. It used to be that you could have a column in a regional newspaper and go on a couple of radio shows. Then it became more national syndication, then the *Today Show* or *Dateline*, and then *Oprah* or *Dr. Phil*. The bar keeps on being raised by publishers who, more and more, want authors who are on higher platforms. It used to be a silver platform, then it became a gold platform and now it's a platinum platform."

"The bar for platforms has been raised to almost absurd heights," according to Encino, California, agent Sharlene Martin. "A whole plethora of good writing is being ignored because it doesn't have the promotional hooks that publishers are now demanding."

Building a Platform

Since a platform has taken on such importance, agents and publishers find themselves advising promising writers who do not have national platforms to go back, build platforms, and then come back and see them.

"If someone doesn't have a platform, I usually tell them that, 'They are before their time,'" Sharlene Martin states. "They're too young, too fresh, they need to spend the next couple of years getting a Web site up, doing public speaking and publishing articles. Volunteer to become an expert by getting yourself in some expert directories and then you'll be ready."

Some basic ways to build a platform are covered in the following sections.

Platform Builder #1: Give Talks Around the Country

This is the most common method. However, "It can be a Catch-22," Santa Monica agent Bonnie Solow observes. "Writers often can't get speaking engagements without a book, and they can't get a book without a platform."

Here's how to get your speaking career off the ground:

- Start locally by approaching civic, community, and religious organizations. Develop a series of talks for the Y, your church, or the Rotary Club and then move up to larger groups and venues. Ask everyone you know to help you find bookings; speak often and work your way up. Make your initial mistakes locally and build a devoted fan base close to home.

■ Hone your craft by taking speaking, voice, or acting lessons or hiring a professional media coach. Then practice, practice, practice.

■ Perfect your presentations by joining Toastmasters and the National Speakers Association.

■ Ask your audiences and your friends to critique your performances and to give you their suggestions. Tape and record your talks and ruthlessly critique yourself.

■ Constantly read, and learn the latest trends and developments so that you can incorporate them into your speeches.

Platform Builder #2: Gain Media Presence

Some of the ways that you can raise your media profile include:

■ Inform members of the media about your appearances and invite them to attend as your guest.

■ Maintain a file of articles about you and your presentations that you can use to get more media coverage.

■ Write a regularly published column, newsletter, or blog. Again, start small or locally and then try to build your exposure.

■ Promote yourself as an expert whom reporters can interview on your particular area of expertise, and regularly appear on television or cable.

Platform Builder #3: Make Use of the Internet

Another effective way to create your platform is becoming involved and building a following as the leader of or an active participant in Internet communities that focus on the subject matter of the book. Starting and leading an online community can position you as an expert; expand your following; and inform you of problems, issues, and developments in your field.

Platform Builder #4: Find Partners

You can enlist support for the book by one or more noncompeting, promotional partners. For example, get a business or nonprofit organization that is excited enough about the book to write a letter that can be added at the end of the proposal. The letter must commit to buying copies of the book, sending the author on a national promotional tour, and/or featuring the author in the organization's advertising or on its Web site and internal media.

Merely pointing out the possibility of getting promotional partners in a proposal will not be convincing. "Without a letter, a promotional partner is only an idea. Publishers want commitments," agent Michael Larsen stresses.

Platform Builder #5: Publish Your Chapters

Get the chapters you have written to work for you. Send them out as articles in order to build your platform.

Robyn Says

"Get your writing out there; build your publishing credentials by submitting your sample chapters as articles to magazines, newsletters, or journals. Having been published will help you attract agents and publishers as well as overcome the lack of a platform, or a weak one.

"In the beginning, I wrote how-to craft books, educational books. They let me get my foot in the door and be taken seriously when I ventured into the trade-book market. I also wrote articles and even volunteered to write an article about good Samaritans in our community to establish my voice as a writer, which I enjoyed.

"Every opportunity that you create matters. Plus, writing is really enjoyable. I wrote those articles not just to get noticed, but because my heart was in it. Find something you love to write about and the rest will take care of itself."

Platform Builder #6: Develop a Great Web Site

Editors check on authors on the Internet; they go to their Web sites to find out who they are, what they've done, and how they present themselves. Editors expect authors to have great Web sites, preferably ones that get lots of hits. They consider it a part of the package that is required of authors today.

Platform Builder #7: Create a Qualitative Survey

Hire a company that conducts surveys to test, support, or document the central theory of your book. Or do it yourself. Run a survey that will demonstrate the need for your book. Conducting the first survey on a subject or a unique aspect of it can establish you as an authority on that subject. It will make both you and your survey newsworthy. The media loves to report on surveys, so a survey will get you ink. If a survey demonstrates a need for your book, your book will be more apt to sell.

Platform Builder #8: Conduct Focus Groups

Focus groups that test your book or its concepts can add credibility and help you build your platform in several ways. For example:

- The information that focus groups provide can show you ways to strengthen your book.
- The answers you receive can boost your stature in your field.
- When eighteen of twenty group members say that they benefited from your program, information, or advice, they become a part of your following and their testimonials can add weight to your platform.

Platform Builder #9: Document Your Success

Build your expertise, legitimacy, and following by providing proof of the success of your approaches. Take before and after photographs to submit with your proposal for your weight-loss book, or diary entries that show that your methods work and the clear benefits they provide.

Get endorsements and testimonials and compile statistics that show that your concepts really work.

"What I know is that you have to have credibility before you can write a book," Stedman Graham, author of *Move Without the Ball: Put Your Skills and Your Magic to Work for You* (Fireside, 2004), points out. "Credibility comes in the form of having a business or organization that demonstrates that you can put something together. The single number-one reason that a publisher selects an author and that people believe the author is worth their time and effort to purchase that book is all about credibility. It also comes back to your passion for the idea, because if you are sincerely passionate about it, then at least it's honorable."

Platform Builder #10: Compile a Names List

Create a list of individuals who would be interested in buying your book. At your appearances, in your articles, or on your Web site, offer free giveaways to people who give you their contact information. Check if similar lists are available through list brokers and investigate the value of purchasing them. Publishers like names lists because they help them target book promotions and they also identify a segment of your potential following.

Platform Alternatives

If you don't have a national platform, some agents can help. Publishing is a relationship and reputation business, and some agents have such great reputations and relationships with editors that the editors will read anything the agents recommend. When they truly believe in a writer, they may put their reputation and relationship on the line by recommending an unplatformed writer's proposal.

New Haven agent Don Gastwirth will send a cover letter to an editor whom he has a special connection with that states, "This is really important to me and I think it should be important to you." Gastwirth cautions, however, "They will only read it once. So, it better be good, because you are only as good as your last submission." Other possibilities for overcoming the lack of a platform include:

Platform Alternative #1: Join Forces

When some agents receive submissions that they like from writers who don't have platforms, they try to pair them with people who do. For example, if an author who wrote a diet book doesn't have a degree in nutrition, they may try to connect him or her with a doctor or a nutritionist. Unfortunately, egos and disputes regarding responsibilities and other problems usually waylay these projects. Also authors with platforms may resist because they don't see the need for a collaborator or they may try to diminish the cowriter's role.

Pairings seem to work best when authors are matched before the actual writing begins. Then they can plan the book together, divide responsibilities, and decide how they will work. Even so, coauthoring can be a difficult and taxing experience.

If you don't have a national platform, consider sharing authorship credit with someone who does. But find a collaborator early in the project, as soon as you can. Besides satisfying the platform requirement, your new partner can improve the content of your book with his or her knowledge, insights, and contacts.

Platform Alternative #2: Plug into an Established Book Series

If a series covers an important subject and has established a brand name, it's built a following. Good examples are the Dummies, Chicken Soup, Everything, and Streetwise series of books. With series, the brand and reputation are what sells and are more important than the writer's platform. Agents can plug good writers who do not have national platforms into these series; however, the writers still must have good credentials, even if they don't need big, impressive platforms.

Platform Alternative #3: Turn to Smaller or Niche Publishers

Although the platform requirement has penetrated all levels of publishing, some smaller and niche publishers remain committed to

Rick Says

"Think locally! Local and regional publishers can present great opportunities for writers. Often, the most important objective should be getting published, getting that initial notch in your belt, being able to say that you are a published author. It is a solid foundation upon which you can extend your platform.

"Small and regional presses can provide you with opportunities to display your writing talent. Look into the local and regional presses in your area, learn what kinds of books they publish, and visit and speak with their staffs. Although they may not publish many books, they may be interested in publishing yours because you live locally. Many small presses are dedicated to writing and writers and are eager to help authors learn their trade and start their careers."

putting out quality books on their subjects. Many of these publishers will take on authors who lack platforms. Attend BookExpo America and introduce yourself to smaller houses and presses—thousands of them exist. Speak with them and examine their publications and lists; see if they could be a good match. Many writers may find it more beneficial to be an important, prized author with a smaller publisher than to be a small, neglected author at a big publishing house.

"When buyers are looking at books on the shelves, they're going to buy the one that seems the most authoritative for the price they're willing to pay," book packager Leanne Chearney of Amaranth declares. "Although the platform requirement has filtered down to smaller publishers, it's still more important to the large publishers; in fact, it's basically required. The only books big publishers want are books that can be blockbusters, books that they think they can break out on the bestseller list. And they don't think they can do that unless the author has a great platform. If you don't need your book to be a blockbuster or if you don't have a great platform, try sending your proposal to smaller publishers that don't place such emphasis on the bestseller list," Chearney advises.

Platform Alternative #4: Hire a Book Publicist

Authors who are willing to hire publicists who specialize in promoting books can neutralize some of the fallout from the fact that they don't have national platforms. Publishers are familiar with the top publicists and how they can boost book sales. Any publicist you hire must be highly regarded by publishers and must, as part of the promotional campaign, build the author's platform.

Platform Alternative #5: Work as a Ghostwriter

Writers tend to fall into two general categories: (1) those whose main objective is to pursue a writing career, and (2) those who want to write to further their careers. If you're in category 1, you can build your writing career by collaborating with or writing for someone in category 2. When the book is published, you will be credited and be a published writer, which is an important step in building a platform. Being a published author opens many doors. Showing agents that your book has been published will increase their confidence that if they take on your project, you can deliver.

Action Steps

1. Explain why publishers want authors with established national platforms.
2. List five ways that you could build a platform.
3. List five platform alternatives.
4. Explain why a Web site can be important to an aspiring writer.
5. Identify five celebrities that you could approach to join forces with you on your book.

Remember:

 The stronger your platform, the greater your chances of attracting an agent. Agents seek writers who have national platforms because they're the authors publishers want. Ways to build a platform include speaking, building a media presence, enlisting promotion partners, putting up a Web site, and developing an extensive list of names.

 If you don't have a platform, consider joining forces with those who do. Or, you can try to plug into an established book series, go with smaller or niche publishers, hire a book publicist, or ghostwrite for others.

CHAPTER 12

"Great things are not done by impulse, but by a series of small things brought together."
Vincent Van Gogh

Rights Involved

THIS CHAPTER WILL COVER:

▶ Bundle of rights
▶ What publishers get
▶ The rights involved

We would like to thank and acknowledge New York City literary attorney Lloyd J. Jassin, copylaw@aol.com, *for his great help in writing and reviewing this chapter and also the following chapter on author/agent agreements.*

WRITING AND PUBLISHING a book creates a number of complex legal rights. When these rights are anticipated and planned for, authors can reap substantial rewards. However, if they are ignored, writers can lose out.

In November 1999, when Chronicle Books published the *Worst-Case Scenario Survival Handbook*, by Joshua Piven and David Borgenicht, few suspected that this one book would give birth to a booming new industry. Since then, *Worst-Case Scenario* books have become a series and new volumes have been spun off on travel, dating and sex, holidays, golf, and more. They have been translated into more than twenty languages and have formed the basis for a TV show, a video game, a board game, postcards, posters, note cards, holiday cards, calendars, address books, and journals. The *Worst-Case Scenario* books and products have taken on a life of their own and have become a commercial franchise.

When authors write books, they're automatically launched into the rights business. The moment authors create a piece of writing, certain exclusive rights arise regarding how that writing can be used. Those rights are called copyright rights and they come into being when authors first express their ideas in a tangible form. *Tangible form* is when the idea is expressed in writing, on tape, film, and so on. As soon as the writing is put into tangible form, no one can copy or distribute it without the writer's consent.

When writers hire agents, they primarily employ them to negotiate for the license or sale of book or volume rights to one or more publishers. Who controls what rights—and for how long—is at the heart of the agent–publisher negotiation. So in this chapter we're going to tell you a little about authors' rights.

> NOTE: *The information that follows in this chapter is provided in this book solely to introduce you to the difficult and confusing area of copyrights and copyright law. It is specifically NOT intended to teach you or to advise you about copyright rights and/or copyright law. Do not attempt in any way to take any action regarding your copyright rights without first obtaining the advice of a copyright attorney!*

Bundle of Rights

Copyrights consist of a bundle of five legal rights. Those rights can be divided and sold to one or more people for different periods of time and for use in different territories or media. Many agents excel at selling authors' rights to publishers, but they may not be expert when it comes to making the most of their clients' other rights.

The five copyright rights are as follows.

1. *The right of reproduction.* This means that when an author writes a book, he or she has the exclusive right to publish, photocopy, download, or otherwise duplicate it. The term *copyright* comes from the words *copy* and *right*. So you, as an author, have the exclusive right to copy the book you write and the writing in it.

2. *The right to make derivative works.* If you write a book, you have the exclusive right to make works based on your book in other formats. For example, condensed versions, revised editions, translations, illustrated versions, and comic-book versions.

3. *The right to distribute the work and to make the first publication.* As the author, you alone have the right to distribute your work to others and to be the first one to publish what you wrote. When you sign with a publisher, you license it to exclusively reproduce and distribute your book.

4. *Right to perform the work.* If you write a book, you also have the exclusive right to recite it publicly or to perform it as a play, dance, or even a puppet show.

5. *The right to display the work.* As the copyright owner, you have the exclusive right to publicly show images of or from your book by means of film, TV, or other device.

So, when you're about to enter into a book contract, think in terms of copyright rights, because your publishing house will! When publishers agree to publish your book, they will want as many rights as they can get for as little as they have to pay. Conversely, you and your agent will try to reserve as many of those rights for yourself and make as much money as you can for the rights you convey to your publisher.

Entering into a publishing contract should not be taken lightly. Potentially, it is a very long-term relationship. If a book is successful, your publisher and you, or your heirs, could be bound together for the life of the copyright. This could mean for the rest of your life plus another seventy years.

"Keep in mind that most publishing contracts are not take-it-or-leave-it propositions; the terms can be negotiated," literary attorney

Lloyd Jassin notes. "However, knowing what to ask for is critical. Use an agent or attorney who understands the parameters of the typical publishing deal to negotiate your contract. Working through an agent or attorney allows you to preserve your creative relationship with your editor."

What Publishers Get

When a publisher buys your book, it usually acquires the exclusive right to reproduce, publish, distribute, and sell it in book or volume form. It also can obtain a number of additional rights that are known as subsidiary rights. Subsidiary rights can include reprint, translation, serialization, film, television, and a host of other rights. See the list at the end of this chapter.

Who Controls What Rights?

"Standardized contracts are powerful negotiation tools," Jassin points out. "Many authors will simply sign what is put in front of them." He cautions authors to understand each right that they're granting the publisher. For example, if a contract grants the publisher "all rights in the work," the author most likely will have assigned his entire copyright to the publisher—including the right to characters, motion picture, television, and merchandising rights.

You don't have to be a well-established author like Stephen King or J. K. Rowling to retain these valuable rights. However, you do have to have an understanding of what your contract says and what is considered standard in the industry. By failing to delete the words "motion picture, television, and radio" rights from your contract, your revenue from these income streams could be reduced by 50 percent or more.

Most writers have little understanding or familiarity with the rights involved in book sales. With the strategic stroke of a pen or proper placement of a cursor, a contract can be much improved.

The Rights Involved

An author's rights fall into two categories: primary and subsidiary (or secondary). The lists below are not all inclusive; naming every right would be too lengthy for our purposes. However, this listing should provide you with a good overall idea of what rights are involved and opportunities that agents should investigate.

Primary Rights

Under most publishing contracts, the basic royalty rate that publishers pay authors is usually payable for sales in the following categories:

A. Hardcover books
B. Trade paperback books (large-format paperback books sold in bookstores)
C. Mass-market sales (small-format paperback books [e.g., 5" × 8"], often sold on spin racks found in supermarkets, drug stores, stationery stores, and airport bookstores)
D. E-book sales

Additional royalty amounts may be paid under:

- *Royalty escalation clauses.* Escalator clauses kick in when specified conditions occur, such as selling a particular number of books or receiving particular awards.
- *Bestseller bonus clauses.* Additional amounts may be added when authors' books are listed on specified bestseller lists.

An important note: Your basic royalty may be reduced for a variety of reasons—some legitimate, others not. A savvy agent or publishing attorney will negotiate on your behalf to get these rates up. Here are typical royalty reductions (all subject to negotiation):

A. *Deep discount and special sales.* Certain booksellers, such as the huge chain stores, demand and receive special discounts. Special sales can be those made to retailers other than booksellers.

B. *Premium sales.* Volume sales made to companies for promotional purposes or for sale with their products. Also, there may be specially tailored versions for particular organizations.

C. *Small printings.* This refers to short-run reprints where maybe 1,500 or 2,500 copies are being reprinted.

D. *Revised editions.* Typically, your publisher has the right to hire someone to revise your book if you are unable or unwilling to do so. Up to 50 percent of your royalties can paid to the person revising your book on the first revision cycle. If not addressed, the original author's split can fall to 10 percent or less by the third revision cycle.

Subsidiary (Secondary) Rights

For the following categories of rights, the standard royalty splits range from 50 percent to 90 percent, depending on the right being sold. Who controls these rights—the agent or the publisher—is often subject to intense negotiation. If the author is unknown, the publisher will more likely control first serialization, foreign translation, and British Commonwealth rights.

A. Book club sales
B. Serialization sales
C. Anthology sales
D. Large-print book edition sales
E. Foreign translation
F. British Commonwealth
G. Future. New technology rights sales
H. Audio rights
I. Motion picture/TV (usually retained by the author)
J. Merchandising (usually retained by the author)

Agents know the markets for subsidiary rights, what these rights are worth and how to go about selling them. They also know when to work or coagent with other agents in specialty areas such as foreign sales and film. In addition, agents will negotiate how publishers and authors split the proceeds from subsidiary rights sales, including the percentages that each will receive.

Appendix E features a publishing contract checklist graciously provided by the Law Offices of Lloyd J. Jassin (*www.copylaw.com*).

Action Steps

1. List the rights an author receives with a copyright.
2. Explain what rights publishers usually acquire when they buy a book.
3. Name the rights included in an author's primary rights.
4. Explain what an escalator clause is.
5. List five subsidiary rights.

Remember:

 When authors create written works, certain exclusive rights arise regarding how that work can be used. Those rights are called copyright rights and they come into being when authors first express their ideas in a tangible form. When the writing is put into tangible form, such as in a writing, a recording, a film, or a work of art, no one can copy or distribute it without the writer's consent.

 When a publisher buys a book, it usually acquires the exclusive right to reproduce, publish, distribute, and sell it in book form. It also can obtain additional rights that are known as subsidiary rights. They can include reprint, translation, serialization, film, television, and a host of other rights. The ownership and financial arrangements regarding the rights stemming from a book should be spelled out in the author/publisher agreement.

CHAPTER 13

"Example is not the main thing in influencing others. It is the only thing."
Albert Schweitzer

Author/Agent Agreements

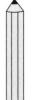

THIS CHAPTER WILL COVER:

► Scams
► The agreement
► Scope of authority
► Duration
► Expenses
► Compensation
► Cancellation
► Payments

EARLY IN THE COURTSHIP, most agents will ask you to sign an author/agent agreement, in which you authorize them to represent you and you agree to pay them for selling your book. Most will ask for an agreement before they put in much work, which is fair. *Caution:* Don't let an agent rush you into signing anything until you understand the legal ramifications and you are absolutely certain that you are comfortable with this person's representing you.

In business, the term *due diligence* means fully investigating all deals or opportunities before getting involved in them. So, before you sign with an agent, do your due diligence. Regrettably, thousands of starry-eyed writers fall prey to dishonest literary agents, book doctors, and subsidy publishers each year.

Scams

Whether it's called a reading fee or a handling fee, just say no! Don't pay an up-front fee to an agent to critique your book.

A predatory agent may act as a "book doctor" or refer you to one, generally for a healthy kickback. While qualified book doctors do exist, they are few and far between. A common scam occurs when an agent promises to represent you provided Book Dr. X edits your book. Of course, the book doctor charges you a large fee, of which the agent usually gets a chunk.

After whipping your manuscript into shape, a conniving agent or book doctor may refer you to a subsidy publisher, also for a kickback. The subsidy or vanity publisher's promotional materials may contain the phrase "joint venture." Beware! The term *joint venture* means that you have to pay to get your book published.

As a general rule, independent and chain bookstores will not touch vanity books. They may show up at online book sites, but the mainstream press will not review them.

Traditional publishers put their own money at risk—not yours. Bona fide publishers pay you a nonrefundable advance against future royalties. A legitimate publisher also pays the cost of producing, manufacturing, and distributing your book. When a publisher risks its own money, it will work to recoup that investment by supporting the book. By contrast, a "joint venture," "subsidy," or "vanity" publisher makes money selling you your own book. At best, these publishers are little more than printers.

Beware of scam artists; they can be slick. They usually come equipped with impressive brochures, get back to you quickly with copious praise, and can't be found in the guidebooks that list publishers. They are the literary equivalent of storefront fortune-tellers who steal money from old ladies.

When seeking to avoid such scam artists, you can take some comfort if a literary agent belongs to the Association of Authors' Representatives (AAR). As we pointed out in Chapter 2, AAR agents may not charge reading, evaluation, and similar fees, and they must follow the

AAR Canon of Ethics and have a track record as an agent to become a member. However, also understand that many reputable agents don't belong to the AAR for a variety of valid reasons.

If an agent expresses interest in your work, ask if he or she is an AAR member. Also, get a list of his or her clients and permission to contact them. Then follow the procedures and ask all the questions that we detailed in Chapter 9, "Finding the Best Agent for You."

The Agreement

The type of agreement that an agent will ask you to sign can vary. Some agencies may require formal, detailed, written contracts whereas others have little more than a letter agreement or memorandum. Rarities, like New Haven agent Don Gastwirth, will work under a handshake agreement. While trust is an essential component of any good relationship, according to attorney Lloyd Jassin, "Ambiguity and open terms are the two key ingredients in litigation soup."

A written agreement is important. If a dispute arises, a well-drafted contract will anticipate it, which could save you a ton of money later on in legal fees. Whatever agreements you make, get them in writing! Memories fade, relationships break down, and unwritten agreements are subject to misinterpretation.

An important note: Letter agreements can be as binding as long, formal contracts. So read every word of any agreement, letter, or memo that a prospective agent asks you to sign. Make sure that you fully understand each and every provision. If you don't, or feel that anything is unreasonable or unfair, speak up. Consult a literary attorney. Ask the agent what he or she means and why it's included and make sure that you can live with both the answer and the agreement.

If an agent's explanation seems to contradict or go beyond what is written in the agreement, ask him or her to write in what he or she explained. If he or she won't, either walk away and take your business elsewhere or have your attorney attempt to renegotiate the terms.

The most important purpose of an author/agent agreement is to clarify the duties and responsibilities of each of the parties, to set out what each is expected to give and receive. A good contract should be fair and reasonable to both parties. A fair contract will help you and your agent build a strong working relationship based on trust, which is what you want with your literary representative.

In virtually all cases, the author/agent agreements that you will be asked to sign were written by or on behalf of the agent. So they may naturally be slanted in the agent's direction. To protect your rights, have the agreement reviewed by an attorney.

> NOTE: *The information on author/agent agreements is intended solely to give you an overview of such agreements and alert you to some of the points they may include. The information that we are providing is not intended to be legal advice of any kind. For such advice and all questions regarding author/agent agreements, consult an attorney.*

Scope of Authority

Although author/agent agreements will differ, they should all cover some basic areas. One of those areas is the agent's scope of authority—in other words, what you in the agreement are giving the agent permission to do on your behalf.

Agents will want the exclusive right to negotiate and sell your book and the subsidiary rights that flow from it. Exclusivity means that if you have an agent and then run across an old girlfriend who works at W.W. Norton at a party and she falls in love with and buys your manuscript, you must give your agent a commission on that sale—even though he had nothing to do with selling it.

When you give an agent exclusive rights, those rights should be confined to one book or literary property, not to everything you write or will write in the future. That way, when you sign an agreement naming an agent as your exclusive sales representative for your fly-fishing book, you can still hire another agency to sell your screenplay to Hollywood. Book agents and theatrical agents tend to specialize.

To make sure that an agent doesn't put you into deals you don't like, include a requirement that the agent must obtain your approval on all offers and that you must sign all agreements. Such a provision is included in both of the sample agreements reproduced in Appendix D at the end of this book. Although a clause requiring the author's consent may not be included in their basic agreements, reputable agents will consent to the addition of this clause.

The language in the contract that you sign with your agent and in the agreement with your publisher should be consistent. Otherwise questions might arise regarding which one prevails.

The Agency Clause

The reason publishers send royalty checks to agents, not authors, is because agents insert a clause in author/publishing contracts requiring them to do so. That clause, the "agency clause," is buried in the author/publishing contract and is usually drafted by agents, not publishers. The fact that it directs publishers to pay all monies due under the contract to agents is all well and good, but sometimes things creep into agency clauses that don't appear in the author/agent agreement.

Worse yet, the agency clause can outright contradict the author/agent agreement. For example, some agency clauses contain language that states the agent has an interest in the work itself, which you don't want. It's what is called an "agency coupled with interest." If you see those words, strike them from the contract.

The agency clause should also not state that the agent has the authority to act on the author's behalf. If the agent has this authority, it can be considered a power of attorney. You wouldn't give your best friend the authority to do whatever he likes with your property, so why give your literary agent the authority to do whatever she likes with your intellectual property? Strike this clause.

Duration

Some agreements run for a particular term or duration; for example, six months, a year, or several years. If many of these agreements are not expressly cancelled prior to expiration, they automatically renew themselves for an additional month term.

If a period of time is specified in an agency agreement, it should be long enough to allow the agent to place the work and negotiate a contract. Conventional wisdom—and the Authors Guild—suggests that short-term (e.g., terminable upon thirty days written notice) agreements are better. If an agent stops returning your calls or otherwise exhibits lack of interest in your book, you want to be able to get out of your contract sooner rather than later.

Agreements that do not run for stated periods of time can be advantageous for authors because the authors, arguably, can cancel them by giving the required notice. For the sake of certainty, nothing should be left to chance. Either state with certainty how long the agreement is to run or, if the contract is of nonspecific length, state how it can be terminated.

Give an agent enough time to do a good job. Pressing for too short of an agreement term can backfire on you. It can force an agent to rush and not fully explore all of the possibilities. Furthermore, if, during negotiations on the agency agreement, the agent feels you are demanding too short a term, he or she might elect not to represent you.

A better approach may be to do your due diligence. Thoroughly check out the agent and make sure that you want him or her to represent you. Then show your confidence in your agent and in your book by allowing him or her to do his or her job.

Termination

Authors should be able to get out of an author/agent agreement sixty or ninety days after giving the agent written notice. Some agents will allow clients to leave on thirty-days' notice, and others, such as Don Gastwirth, take the position that clients should be free to go when they wish.

Remember, as we noted with the duration of an author/agent agreement, requesting too short an out could work against you. It may not provide much of an incentive for an agent to represent you if you won't give him or her sufficient time to develop and sell your project.

Also watch out for provisions that require you to give an agent written notice in order to cancel the agreement or the agreement will automatically renew. Usually, these clauses require you to give written notice to the agent thirty or sixty days before the agreement is scheduled to end. So if you are thinking of switching agents when your agreement runs out, check for this clause and how much written notice you have to give.

If an agent begins negotiating with a publisher during the term of an author/agent agreement but the deal doesn't conclude until after the contract has expired, the agent should still be entitled to receive his or her fee. Some agency agreements contain a provision that states that if an editor who is currently considering the manuscript doesn't make an offer within a specified length of time (e.g., ninety days) after termination, the sale is not commissionable.

Authors may outgrow their agents or the relationship can become strained. Even though Agent A sold your first novel, you may feel a new broom will sweep cleaner. Dicey issues can crop up if you terminate your old agent and hire someone new to represent you.

According to attorney Lloyd Jassin, if the old agent is the agent of record on one or more of your publishing contracts, you can try to have your old agent return any unsold rights to your book to you. If your agent is unwilling to do so, other options include splitting the commissions between your old and new agents.

If you and your agent part company, don't hesitate to ask the agent to sign a letter directing your publisher to pay all of the proceeds from your book to you—minus the agent's commission, which would be paid directly to him or her.

Accounting Provisions

Literary attorney Lloyd Jassin suggests that authors include an accounting provision in their agreements with their agents. Under this provision, the agent would agree to give the author, within X days of termination of the agreement:

■ A list of all submissions that the agent made.
■ A list of rejections received.
■ A closing memo describing the status of the book and the agent's efforts to shop it.

Including this requirement can prevent an agent from trying to cash in on or take credit for a deal that you subsequently close, which he or she didn't broker.

Expenses

A well-drafted agency agreement should address the issue of expenses. Some agents don't pass along out-of-pocket expenses, but most do. Expenses can be paid as you go along or taken out of first proceeds, such as your advance. Typical expenses include those incurred for photocopying proposals and manuscripts, bound galleys, and finished books for subsidiary rights submissions. They also include postage, overnight delivery, messenger fees, and wire transfer fees.

As we stated earlier, it's wise to include a provision stating that you must approve expenses in excess of a certain amount.

Compensation

Today, agents typically receive a 15 percent commission for representing you and 15 to 25 percent for the sale of foreign translation rights. The spread usually depends on whether a subagent or coagent is used.

When a subagent is actually involved, a 20 percent commission is now considered the norm. Therefore, the two agents together can collect no more than the 20 percent commission you agreed to in the author/agent agreement.

Funds

Author/agent agreements should state when the author will be paid. Lloyd Jassin, Esq., includes a provision in his clients' agreements that requires payment to be sent to the author within ten days of the agent's actual receipt of proceeds. This gives agents plenty of time to deposit the checks and for them to clear.

Similarly, agents should also report and send authors prompt statements when they make deals or receive moneys from subsidiary rights. They should also not delay sending statements and notices that they receive from the publisher. Again, sending these items to you within ten days of receipt is reasonable.

Most author/agent agreements don't require the agents to maintain a trust account for the funds they receive on behalf of their clients, but they should. Since your agent will be holding money that belongs to you, your money should be held separately from the agent's other accounts. Separate accounts avoid the commingling of funds and provide a clear paper trail in the event problems arise. Since this clause is usually hard to enforce, ask for the right to inspect the agent's records and accounts.

Other Considerations

Be on the alert for and strike any clause in either your author/agent agreement or the author/publishing agreement that gives an agent any ownership interest in your book. Your agent is your representative, not a partial owner of your book. If an agent has an ownership interest in your book, he or she could make claims against you for the life of the copyright on the book, which is your life plus seventy years, even if he or she no longer represents you.

If your book goes out of print and you have the right to buy it back from the publisher, which you exercise, the agent could claim an ownership interest in the book. Then you would be forced to negotiate with the agent and buy out his or her interest.

Also consider adding another clause that states how long your agent will have to place your book with another publisher after it goes out of print. If the book is not placed within the allotted time, the agent's right to commissions on the work should cease.

Your agreement with your agent should specify the state where the agreement will be construed and the law that it will be subject to. For example, it should say that it's subject to the laws of the state of _____. Whenever possible, make the agreement subject to the law in the state most convenient to you.

Also consider inserting a clause that all disputes must be resolved by binding arbitration, which can dispose of problems less expensively and more quickly. However, insist that the arbitrators have knowledge of publishing law.

Action Steps

1. Explain what the term *due diligence* means.
2. State why it's important that an author approve all offers his or her agent receives.
3. What is an automatic renewal clause?
4. Why is it important for agents to hold their clients' funds in separate bank accounts?
5. List two reasons why it can be desirable for writers to have all disputes with agents resolved by binding arbitration.

Remember:

 Agents will usually require potential clients to sign an author-agent agreement. In this agreement, the client authorizes the agent to represent him or her and agrees to pay the agent for selling his or her books. Some of the issues that should be covered in the agreement include the scope of the agent's authority, what he or she is authorized to do on your behalf.

 Other considerations are how long the agreement is in force, how and when it can be terminated and the compensation and expense reimbursement the agent is entitled to receive. The agreement should also state when the author is to be paid.

CHAPTER

14

"I've given my memoirs far more thought than any of my marriages. You can't divorce a book."

Gloria Swanson

Leaving an Agent

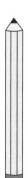

THIS CHAPTER WILL COVER:

▶ Contacting your agent
▶ Terms and cancellation
▶ Notice

LIKE MARRIAGES, author/agent relationships fail. As in marriages, offspring can be involved in an author/agent relationship and can be the source of thorny problems. With authors and agents, the offspring are the writers' books and the rights that flow from them. After break-ups, agents are generally entitled to share in the proceeds of deals they negotiated when they represented their clients.

Even after you leave an agent, he or she may be entitled to compensation for subsequent sales whether or not he or she represented you on those sales. For example:

1. Agent A sold your book.
2. You then terminated the agency agreement with Agent A.
3. You hired Agent B.
4. Agent B then sold your rights to make a video game based on your book.

5. Agent A could be entitled to compensation on Agent B's video rights sale.

It 'can get very tricky!

> NOTE: *Leaving an agent can be a complex and costly matter involving numerous rights. Since it involves ending a legal relationship, an attorney should handle it. The information in this chapter is not intended to provide legal advice, but is given solely to alert you to some of the general problems that may arise when you and your agent decide to part. In the event you wish to leave an agent, SEE AN ATTORNEY for legal guidance and advice.*

Contact Your Agent

Authors frequently decide to leave agents because the agents have not sold their books. Since these relationships have not been productive for either party, these splits can be amicable and relatively cut-and-dried.

Some authors terminate an agent relationship too soon. Selling a book takes time. Dr. Ava Wilensky, an aspiring writer, suggests, "Give your agent a chance. If you are lucky enough to get an agent, don't second-guess him or her. Agents want to sell your book as much as you do. They don't make any money unless you do! Don't give up on them and they are likely not to give up on you."

However, if you are certain that ending an author/agent relationship is necessary, consult with your attorney. Decide whether you or your attorney should contact your agent to discuss the matter. If you contact the agent, try to resolve all outstanding issues. Discuss every work he or she may be handling and what stage he or she is at with all rights involved.

When you and your agent come to an understanding, ask him or her to send you a letter confirming that the relationship will end on a certain date and enumerating all matters in which he or she is entitled to share in the proceeds, if any. Settle the amount of any expenses that you might owe and agree to send reimbursement when you receive the agent's letter.

If the agent isn't entitled to any future proceeds, ask him or her to state so in the letter. This can be handy if you're planning to switch agents, because other agents may not be willing to represent you until you and your existing agent have cleared the slate.

Some agents are impossible to reach. They may not return your calls or give you updates. They may even be avoiding you because they sense that you're planning to leave. In addition, your relationship with your agent may have become strained or even contentious. When these or other difficulties arise, contact an attorney and have him or her handle the split.

If you decide to leave after your agent has negotiated, or is in the process of negotiating, sales, more complex problems may be involved.

"If your agent doesn't represent the type of book you want to write, discuss your options. Some authors have more than one agent. They may have one for nonfiction or fiction, but if that agent doesn't also handle children's books, they should be able to hire an agent who specifically handles children's books.

"To avoid potential conflicts and make sure you are totally clear with your agent, specify in your author/agent agreement the genre of books your agent will handle for you. If you want to write different types of books, be up-front with your agent about your intentions.

"If your agent doesn't feel one of your ideas is worth his or her time, get him or her to give you written permission to sell it directly. Don't let an idea you believe in die just because your agent isn't behind it or doesn't sell that type of book. It is always important to listen to your agent and value his or her feelings, but consider your overall goals and don't postpone your dreams."

In such situations, the author/agency agreements, if they exist, usually govern both parties' rights. Again, contact your lawyer and let him or her handle the matter.

Terms and Cancellation

In the previous chapter on author/agent agreements, we discussed cancellation of the author/agency relationship. If you haven't read that chapter, please go back, read it and pay special attention to the section entitled "Termination."

When you have signed an author/agent agreement, it usually controls:

- What both you and the agent must do to terminate your relationship.
- The agents' right to compensation after the relationship has ended.

Check your agreement to see what it states and follow it precisely regarding any notice that you are required to give. As we mentioned in the prior chapter, you may be required to give written notice (1) if the author/agent agreement runs for a specific term, such as one or two years, and automatically renews itself or (2) if the agreement is not for a stated duration but requires you to give prior written notice of your intent to terminate within a stated time.

Rick Says

"If you are required to give an agent notice that you intend to terminate your author/agent agreement, be sure to keep a copy of the notice you send. Request a return receipt that will verify that the notice was delivered. When you get the signed delivery receipt, attach it to your copy of the notice and keep them both in your records. They could prove valuable."

Notice

Notice to an agent that you want to terminate your author/agent agreement should contain certain basic items. Ask your attorney to prepare it. The notice should include:

- A statement that you wish to terminate the relationship. However, don't go into your reasons for wanting to leave.
- The precise date that the relationship will cease. Be sure that the termination date is within the time period called for in your author/agent agreement.
- Instructions that your agent not make any further submissions of your work.
- Instructions to your agent not to begin negotiations on any additional matters, including the sale of any of your rights.

Also request an accounting. Instruct your agent to send you a list of all the submissions he or she made while representing you and a list of all rejections received. Also ask for a statement describing the current status of your book. Get a list of any negotiations that are currently under way as well as of the agent's efforts to shop your book and any of your rights.

Action Steps

1. Explain why it is essential for an attorney to handle the termination of your relationship with your agent.
2. What rights can an agent still retain after he or she no longer represents you?
3. What should a notice to terminate your relationship with your agents state?
4. When you send a notice to terminate your relationship with your agent, what should you keep?

5. Explain why it may be advisable for you to get a final accounting from an agent you're leaving.

Remember:

 When you want to end your relationship with your agent, consult with your attorney before you act. Numerous legal rights may be involved. Decide whether you or your attorney will contact the agent to discuss the matter. If it's you, try to resolve all outstanding issues. Discuss every work he or she may be handling and what stage he or she is at with all rights involved.

 If you and your agent come to an understanding, ask the agent to send you a letter confirming that the relationship will end as of a certain date and enumerating all matters in which he or she is entitled to share in the proceeds, if any. Settle the amount of any expenses that you might owe and agree to send reimbursement when you receive the agent's letter.

"If we encounter a man of rare intellect, we should ask him what books he reads."
Ralph Waldo Emerson

What Agents Hate

THIS CHAPTER WILL COVER:

▶ Agents' dislikes
▶ The top twenty-five

IN OUR INTERVIEWS, we asked literary agents to tell us what prospective clients do that turns them off. Since it's crucial for writers not to alienate agents, we thought that the agents' responses would help them in two major situations: (1) when they approach and speak with agents who might represent them and (2) when they actually work with agents.

Frankly, the size of the list of agents' dislikes surprised us. We didn't expect so many items to be included, so we boiled them down to the top twenty-five. When we compiled this list, we examined each of the entries and they all seemed reasonable, understandable, and easy for writers to avoid or correct.

The fact that agents have so many gripes graphically drummed home to us the message of just how much agents judge and evaluate writers. When writers try to get an agent, they are asked to run a difficult course, and run it under a microscope. Although the level of scrutiny that writers receive is huge, it is definitely surmountable. However, it may take some adjustments and work.

Read the following items that agents dislike and alter your approaches accordingly. Hopefully, the changes you make will improve your chances of convincing the agent you want to represent you and will help you work better and more productively.

In compiling this list, we added each entry in the order we received it. So the order that appears below does not indicate priority or higher importance.

Agents hate the following items:

#1: Lack of commitment

This refers to writers who want to do as little as possible. For example, some writers will say, "Do you really think I need to write a sample chapter?" or "Do I really need to explain the uniqueness of my treatment?"

A proposal has to be great because when you pitch an editor, at least fifty other people will be trying to get that same editor's attention because they want that editor to buy their project. So if you don't put forth your best effort, you're cheating yourself and wasting the agent's time. Writing and selling a book is hard, time-consuming work; it requires dedication and a full commitment.

#2: Inquiries that show that writers have not done their homework

This complaint usually fell into two categories: (1) submissions that are not the type of books an agency accepts and (2) submissions that are not specifically addressed.

Agents repeatedly told us that writers send submissions for novels when they don't handle fiction, or writers send proposals or manuscripts when the agents accept only query letters. Do your homework. Save everyone time and effort by checking the guidebooks and agents' Web sites and learning what types of books they represent.

Submissions that are not specifically addressed are generally sent to "Dear Agent," the agency, or "To Whom It May Concern." These submissions look like form letters. Address all correspondence to a particular individual and make sure that you spell that person's and the agency's name correctly.

#3: Unwillingness to promote a book

As we've so frequently mentioned, a writer's ability and willingness to promote his or her book is essential to agents and publishers. Few nonfiction books can be successful if they're not energetically promoted. Promoting a book can be grueling, and some writers are shocked when agents and editors tell them everything they are expected to do. If you're unwilling or unable to promote your book, discuss it with your agent as soon as possible to identify efforts that you can make and find ways to do those promotional tasks that didn't seem possible.

#4: Writers who don't ask about and follow protocol

Agents have clear protocols that they want their clients to follow. The protocol for every agent can differ. One agent may want you to talk directly with the editor who is debating whether to buy your book, whereas another may want you to stay away when he or she is negotiating a deal. Find out how you can assist your agent. Let the agent take the lead, and he or she will guide you to the next steps. Never call an editor to find out if he or she received the proposal that your agent asked you to send.

#5: Authors who insist that they must receive unrealistically high advances

Writers may ask agents to guarantee that they will get advances of at least a specified amount. Frequently, the numbers they demand are not realistic and have no reasonable basis. Agents are expert at evaluating what books are worth, and since they receive a percentage of the proceeds, they usually try to squeeze out the top dollar.

#6: Authors who try to be all things to all people

Agents and editors prefer tightly focused books. They told us that a writer's audience actually expands the tighter the focus of the book is.

An author cannot be all things to all people. For instance, a writer may think that the market for her children's book is ages four to fourteen, but four-year-olds want different books than fourteen-year-olds do. A diet book focused on young adults, for example, could sell better than a book that tries to appeal to all readers.

#7: Bad attitudes, or a feeling of superiority

Agents complained that writers offend them when they say, "I've written this book, it's brilliant and you have to have it." Agents are also turned off by writers who compare themselves to literary legends or say that their book is the equivalent of or better than bestsellers, great books, or classics. They also complained about writers who toot their own horn artificially, without solid reason. Having confidence is important for writers, but agents know that when most blowhards try to promote their books, they can annoy audiences.

Unless you have good, verifiable reasons, don't claim that the market for your book is exceptionally broad. If you think that your book will actually be the next *Chicken Soup*, dig up facts and figures to prove it.

Similarly, don't claim that your book will create the next bestselling series. "If a book has a series potential, the publisher will figure that out. Your goal in a proposal should be to sell this work; to get them excited about this book and you as the author," New Jersey agent John Willig advises.

#8: Lazy writers who submit sloppy work

If you send a letter or e-mail, run spell-check. It takes no time, and misspellings offend professionals who work with writing. Most agents will not consider queries littered with spelling errors, poor punctuation, or bad grammar; it tells them that a writer is not willing to put the time in to carefully read and edit his or her book. When agents receive sloppy submissions, they tend to think that the writers will deliver books loaded with errors and problems and that the writers themselves will be aggravating to work with.

#9: Writers who don't trust their agents' advice

Agents are professionals; they know the publishing business and the literary market. They generally know more about what editors want and need than writers do. Also, they usually see the big picture better. Some writers may feel that agreeing to what their agents suggest would compromise their values, but agents generally know the best way to proceed. It seems counterproductive to hire and pay an expert and not listen to his or her advice!

An example of how things should work: A writer who had an offer from a small division of a major publisher for very little money contacted Santa Monica agent Bonnie Solow before he signed. She loved the book, but saw that if it had a complete, page-one rewrite, she could sell it for a large amount. She explained her feelings to the writer, and he agreed and rewrote the book in accordance with her directions. Solow then sold the book to a major publisher for many times the amount the writer had originally been offered.

#10: Control freaks

Agents do not like to work with clients who are not willing to change proposals, manuscripts, or strategies that can improve a book or its ability to sell. The best authors are those who are willing to listen and are open to their agents' advice. Although agents aren't the end all and be all, they are professionals, and selling books is their business. They have experience and knowledge and can bring a certain perspective to a project that authors may not have.

#11: Writers who don't inform agents of their background and credentials

Some writers who don't have credentials deliberately leave them out for fear of being rejected. However, many others who have amazing credentials also leave them out because they are modest or are not impressed by their own accomplishments. People who blow their own horns are often the ones who don't have credentials. Conversely, individuals with tremendous knowledge and experience in their fields often tend to take that knowledge for granted. They say, "Oh, it's no big deal." Usually, they're in a universe with people who are brilliant and may have even more impressive credentials.

#12: Not telling agents a project's history
It's really important to let agents know:

- If you've simultaneously submitted your work to multiple agents or if the agent is the only agent looking at it.
- The history of the project to date. Has it been shopped to editors or agents? If so, to whom and what happened?

Some authors don't reveal that the book has already gone to twenty publishers. In these cases, an agent may spend time reading, editing, or developing the project and then unknowingly submit it to editors who have already rejected it.

Don't be afraid to tell an agent that your book has been rejected. Agents frequently take on books that have been shopped and rejected. They may work on them editorially, fixing them up, and some have sold for sizable amounts. Writers should also inform their agents about all changes or revisions they've made since the book was rejected.

#13: Writers who don't contact their agents when problems arise
Frequently, when problems crop up, writers become frustrated and dissatisfied. However, had they contacted their agents, the agents might have explained the situation and helped them find ways to resolve it. Agents can provide creative second opinions. They usually have extensive experience in publishing, and frequently they are accomplished editors. They can also be a writer's best advisor.

#14: Writers who say, "There is no competition for this book"
Rarely does a book have no competition. It's okay to say, "There is no competition precisely like this" and then point out how your book differs. List the closest or most analogous books and state how yours

differs and is better. When writers claim that their books are without competitors, it tells agents that the writers didn't do the hard, basic research to identify and distinguish the closest books. It also makes them think that the writers won't do the necessary research to write a solid book.

#15: Writers who call their agent too much

Agents are busy; if you call them constantly, you'll drive them crazy. So limit your calls, create an agenda for the calls you make, and while it's nice to schmooze and talk now and then, keep in mind that they are running busy operations.

Many agents who are sole proprietors don't have staffs, so they do most office tasks themselves. Find out when it will be convenient for them to speak with you, and schedule a phone conference at a time that will work for you both.

#16: Lack of writing skill

Some people simply don't have the ability to write a publishable book. Frequently, they have so much invested in writing the book that they don't realize that they need professional help. These writers may not be open to constructive advice or guidance or they may have too much ego involvement in the project to see it realistically.

Fortunately, many writing professionals can be hired to help these writers.

#17: Arrogance

Some writers believe that they know more about the publishing industry than their agents do, when they actually know very little about it. When some individuals read an article or two or a book about the publishing world, they begin to think of themselves as authorities on it. While it's important for writers to know and understand the book business, it's foolish and arrogant for them to believe that their knowledge is equivalent or superior to that of professionals who have had careers in publishing.

#18: Writers expressing how much others liked their book

Agents do not want to know about how much others liked a book, unless those others are (1) celebrities or published authors and (2) willing to endorse the book. Friends, family, and colleagues mean well and they may actually love your book. However, they don't always tell writers the hard truth, and they're not usually knowledgeable about what it takes to get an agent or to get a book published.

#19: Not revealing what a book is about

Some writers don't disclose what their books are about and simply state that they are good. Simply saying that a book is good is not sufficient to motivate an agent to look at a manuscript. Agents need more information, including what the topic and premise are, in order to decide if the book is something they wish to consider. So tell them up front and save everyone valuable time.

#20: "Idea-a-day" authors

Don't constantly call your agent to run your latest book idea by her or him. Try not to wear your agent out by barraging him or her with more ideas than he or she can digest. Think your ideas through before you call, then focus and present them in an organized fashion. Agents appreciate authors who respect their time and don't continually use them as sounding boards for unformulated ideas. Although brainstorming can be productive, it can take time that your agent can't spare.

#21: Too many gimmicks and not enough content

Agents want projects that have substance, not cute or clever ideas that soon become tired or old. Occasionally, an inventive stylistic approach or format will work, but generally it's far better to write books that have solid content behind them. If you like and/or excel at being inventive, provide inventive substance, not just fluff.

#22: Receiving samples and novelties

We found mixed reactions on this peeve. Some agents will scarf down those cookies that you baked from the recipes in your pastry cookbook, but others may be watching their weight or feel that you're trying to bribe them. Before you send such items, do a little homework. Check with your agent or his or her staff to find out their policy. If you get the green light, send only what is appropriate, what fits your book and really represents its personality. If you send bones to an agent along with your proposal for your book on the wisdom of dogs, don't be surprised if she doesn't bite.

#23: Submissions that don't deliver what they promise

Authors will say that their books are funny, heartwarming, and shocking, but they don't submit material that exhibits those qualities. Agents need concrete evidence that your book is indeed funny, informative, or innovative. If you can't prove that you will provide what you promise, you will have no credibility and, probably, no agent.

#24: Authors who forget that agents have private lives

Some authors are demanding and insensitive with agents; they call them ten times a day, on holidays, after hours, before hours, and even on weekends. Agents are not on call 24/7. They are not your shrink or your babysitter; they have families, lives of their own, and clear working hours. Find out the best times to call, and if they're out of the office, don't overload their e-mail or answering machines if it can wait.

#25: Writers who call and pitch

Agents are busy and they're not looking for salespeople. They're looking for writers. Although they screen calls, some stragglers slip through. Usually, agents' Web sites tell writers exactly what to submit; however, many writers insist on calling and trying to pitch their books over the phone. Their pitches waste agents' time and can irritate them. Agents are reluctant to get involved with writers who don't learn about their policies and follow them.

Remember:

 Writers can turn off agents in lots of ways, such as when they lack commitment, submit inquiries without doing their homework, and are not willing to promote their books. Agents also hate when writers don't follow protocol, expect unrealistic advances, or submit sloppy work.

 Agents bristle when writers tell them how much others like their book. Only tell them about praise when it's from celebrities or published authors who are willing to endorse the book. They will also avoid or drop writers who call them too much, don't follow their advice, or don't deliver what they promised. Idea-a-day authors and those who pitch more gimmicks than substance will cause their agents to not return their calls.

"Writing is an exploration. You start from nothing and learn as you go."

E.L. Doctorow

Summing Up

THIS CHAPTER WILL COVER:

▶ Agents' role
▶ Be ready
▶ Queries
▶ Be realistic
▶ Don't be discouraged

THANK YOU FOR reading this book, and congratulations for getting to this concluding chapter. We hope the information that we have provided will assist you in finding an agent and getting your book published.

Finding the right literary agent can be like searching for a needle in a haystack or looking for the right mate. It may involve many wrong turns, detours, and dead ends. However, the journey can also be short and well worth it, because your agent can be the most significant person in your literary career.

Finding a great agent who supports you, believes in your work, and mentors you in the book-writing process is a gift. It also can be a win/win situation, because the agent's investment could pay off big-time for you both. Some books clearly win as a result of an agent's passion and perseverance, while others find their way to a publisher because of the author's dedication.

Hiring a literary agent to represent you can definitely fast-forward your writing career. And it can also help you build a long, successful life as an author. However, getting an agent isn't always easy, and getting the right agent may be even more complex.

Fortunately, literary agents differ: Their likes, dislikes, tastes, and ways of operating vary. Some may be easy to approach, whereas you can't get near others. Many agents are devoted to writing, books, and ideas, while their counterparts may care only about your platform and promotion plan. Still others may have rigid, lofty, and unyielding requirements, while some may be looser, more open, and more willing to gamble.

For every rule or requirement, exceptions exist. After twenty agents pass on your book, one may absolutely adore it . . . and one agent who believes in you may be all it takes.

The most important prerequisite in your search for an agent is knowing what you're doing. Arm yourself with information, as much as you can find. Learn about agents in general and individual agents in depth. Develop a plan and stick with it.

Before we end this book, we would like to reiterate some points that we think could help you along. We think that they are essential to your search for an agent, and will help you work with agents more productively. They are:

Understand the Role of Agents

To find the best agent, it's important to understand the role of agents and how they work. Agents are the ultimate publishing-industry insiders; they know publishing from every perspective, inside and out. They work both sides of the street. Many publishers don't accept unsolicited or unagented inquiries, proposals, and manuscripts, so being represented by an agent may be your only opportunity to get in a traditional publisher's door.

Literary agents cultivate close, long-standing relationships with editors and key people at publishing companies. Agents know what editors want, what is on their lists, what publishers like, and what they need. They also know which editors to approach and when and how to pitch them.

Since publishing is their business, agents understand the market. They know what books are selling, who is buying them, and the price they are paying. They are also up on the trends and developments in the industry, so they know what's hot and how to tap into that market. Agents are constantly in contact with editors. In an industry with great turnover, they know when editors move, where they go, and who, if anyone, replaces them.

Most important, agents understand that book publishing is a business—a big, profit-driven business. They realize that publishers must make money in order to survive and that virtually every major decision in publishing reflects a business- and profit-oriented goal. Therefore, they act as screeners for publishing houses and submit only those book proposals that they think will sell.

An agent's primary job is to represent and protect his or her clients' interests, which usually involves selling the book and negotiating the contract and fees. Many agents have become literary managers, and as such they help build their clients' careers. After a book has been sold, an agent monitors the publisher's actions to make sure it is keeping its bargains and doing its best to promote and distribute the book. The agent also looks for future opportunities for the writer, including those for follow-up books, additional printing runs, added publicity, and other benefits.

In return for their services, agents receive a commission on the income generated from the book deals they make. They are paid a percentage of the royalties writers receive and of sales of authors' subsidiary rights. Since agents are only paid when their clients' books sell, they are exceptionally selective in whom they decide to represent.

Some agents represent a variety of authors who write about many different fields, but others specialize. Some literary agencies have agents who specialize in different areas. If an agent or an agency doesn't handle your type of book, they usually can refer you to someone who does. And their recommendations can make a difference.

Be Ready

Many writers make the mistake of trying to get an agent before they're ready. Often, they have such strong belief in their project and such passion for it that they expect everyone else to respond on the same level. In many cases, writers' ideas have not been fully crystallized and the writers haven't done their basic research and don't have a compelling written submission ready to send when an agent requests it.

Before you approach an agent, fully think through the concept and approach of your book. Go to libraries, bookstores, and online to learn how others have handled the topic. If you can't find anything directly on point, find everything similar or close. Identify how your book or concept differs, why it is better and what it will provide that others do not. Find your book's special niche.

Create a plan of attack and stick to it. Remember, your book project is the equivalent of beginning a new business, so go after it forcefully. Becoming an author takes work, lots of hard work, but good planning, organization, and having the discipline to conscientiously implement your plan can facilitate it. Make yourself more attractive to agents by having a platform in place. Create a dynamic Web site, speak frequently about your subject, lead and participate in classes and workshops. Build a following. Make yourself an authority, write articles and reviews and build a hefty mailing list. Although we can't all be the next Deepak Chopra, Nigella Lawson, or John Gray, an agent will want to see that you have a following and the experience, energy, and drive to vigorously promote a book.

Do Your Research

Learn about agents by researching them. Agents are professionals and, as such, they prefer to deal with informed clients. It makes their job easier because they don't have to explain every little point. When clients bring knowledge to the table, it lifts the level of the author/agent relationship, usually making it more efficient and productive. Find out who represented authors of books similar to yours and books you like. Check all the guidebooks and online guides. Speak with other writers and people who work in bookstores, libraries, and publishing. Ask them if they know the names of agents you could contact.

When you get the names of agents, look them up on their Web sites and in the guides. See what kinds of books and authors they represent. Do they handle books like yours and by authors you know, have read, or who may have influenced you? Review their submission requirements and be sure that you can give them exactly what they want.

Write your book proposal so you can make it available the moment an agent shows interest. That way, you won't have to work insanely to throw a proposal together. Be prepared: Have the proposal and sample chapters written. Ask your friends and colleagues to critique them. Have teachers, writers, editors, or others who know writing review them for spelling, grammar, and punctuation errors. Consider hiring a professional editor to review anything you plan to submit.

Make Your Queries Perfect

Your query letter or e-mail is usually critical in interesting an agent; it may be the most important item you ever write. Although agents are inundated with queries, they're always searching for nuggets and new discoveries—one of which could be your book.

Before you send a query, check each agent's Web site. Be sure that you understand exactly what the agent wants and deliver it. The primary purpose of a query is to ask if an agent is interested in learning more about your book. In most cases, it provides the first impression of you and your book that an agent will receive. Like most first impressions, your query can be crucial . . . so make it fabulous! Work on it until it's perfect.

Capture the agent's interest by clearly demonstrating that you're professional, disciplined, and articulate and that you have a great idea for a book that will sell. In your query, describe the following:

- What your book is about.
- Whom your book will benefit.
- How your book will benefit them.
- The size of your audience.
- Why you are qualified to write this book.

Before you send your query, check every detail and be sure that it contains exactly what the agent wants. Don't send it until it's perfect!

Be Realistic

Clarify your expectations. Identify exactly what you would want an agent to do for you. Do you want an agent to sign you with a large, well-known publisher and obtain at least a $30,000 advance? Or would you prefer a more prestigious house, one with wide international distribution, or a publisher that will give your book time to find its niche?

Discuss your expectations with prospective agents. Writers often have unrealistic hopes, and agents can ground them, which may prevent major disappointments. When you and your agent understand each other's expectations, it improves communication and helps to build a more productive working relationship.

Also define your priorities. Usually, getting your book published is the most important consideration. So listen to your agent's advice and be open to his or her suggestions. Agents know and understand publishing, so their recommendations can help your book get sold to the right publisher. Plus, they have a direct financial interest in your book's sale and success.

Don't Be Discouraged

Although the process of finding the right agent can be difficult and discouraging, don't give up. Making the right connection can be worth every hurdle you face. During your darkest moments, stay on track. Keep your focus, stay with your plan, and keep telling yourself that many have done it and you can too.

Believe in yourself, believe in your ideas, and believe in your book. Get good advice and be open to constructive suggestions that can help. Be willing to make changes because, often, that's all it may take. Remain patient, keep reading and writing, stay with it, and make it work.

The key to becoming a successful author is believing in yourself, in your work and in being prepared for every aspect of the process. If you depend on an agent to make it happen, it may never occur. However, if you follow our suggestions and proceed carefully and diligently, your book could find a home. The key is in the heart of the writer. So be passionate, be prepared, and continue to persevere.

Appendix A
Glossary of Publishing Terms

PUBLISHING INDUSTRY PERSONNEL tend to speak in short-hand that they assume everyone understands, which is not always the case. When they talk about books and publishing, they can completely lose you. For example, publishing people constantly refer to "trade books," which can leave industry outsiders scratching their heads.

Unless you ask for clarification, important information about your proposal or book deal can sail completely over your head. Familiarize yourself with the following lingo so when you chat with agents and publishing personnel, you can understand what they're saying and be sure that you're both on the same page.

ABA

See American Booksellers Association.

acquisitions editor

An editor at a publishing company who has the responsibility to obtain and screen manuscripts that the house may wish to publish.

advance

This term is used in two ways, to mean

(1) An advance against royalties, which is the amount that a publishing company pays an author on signing a book contract and prior to publication, and

(2) The number of copies of a book ordered from the publisher prior to the book's publication.

advance copies

The version of a book that is sent to reviewers and booksellers prior to publication. They are usually not the final version, may have a different cover, and may not be fully corrected.

agent

See literary agent.

ALA

See American Library Association.

American Booksellers Association (ABA)

The major industry association for U.S. booksellers. Its annual trade show, BookExpo, is where people in the industry display and learn about new publications and products.

American Library Association (ALA)

The oldest and largest library association in the world. Has members in academic, public, school, government, and special libraries.

Association of American Publishers (AAP)

The industry association for large book publishers.

auction

The process in which publishers bid to obtain the rights for books.

backlist

Titles that publishers released prior to the current season and are continuing to sell.

backmatter

Material provided in a book after the text. Can include appendixes, glossaries, recommended books, and resource lists.

blurbs (cover copy)

Short quotes from successful authors, reviewers, or publications in praise of an author or book. Usually placed on the front and back covers and first few pages to promote the book.

boilerplate
Standard contractual clauses or language. Generally, they are subject to negotiation and change.

book clubs
Groups that sell and send designated books to their members at regular intervals and at reduced prices.

BookExpo America (BookExpo)
The mammoth annual trade show sponsored by the American Booksellers Association that is attended by thousands of publishing companies and publishing-related businesses.

book proposal
See proposal.

Books in Print
An R. R. Bowker publication that lists books currently in print. Generally available in library reference departments.

bulk sales
Books sold in volume to a single purchaser at a discounted price.

coagent
An agent who works with a writer's agent usually on specialized

subsidiary rights such as film, foreign language translations, and television rights. Also known as a subagent.

copyediting
Review of manuscripts for errors in spelling, grammar, punctuation, syntax, and meaning. Copyediting is a part of the publishing process that is usually done by professional editors at the publisher's expense.

copyright
The federally protected property rights granted to creators that control how a book and other works may be used by others.

co-op ads (cooperative advertising)
Advertisements run by booksellers that are partially paid by publishers to promote their books.

cover copy
See blurbs.

cover letter
A transmittal letter or e-mail sent to an agent, editor, or publisher with a book proposal, manuscript, or other material.

critique fees
See evaluation fees.

dust jacket
See jacket.

earned out

An author has earned out when he or she has earned royalties in an amount that equals the advance against royalties that the publisher previously paid him or her.

evaluation fees

The charges made by agents to read and critique writers' book proposals, manuscripts, or other materials.

first serialization

The publication of selected portions of a book in periodicals prior to the book's publication. *See also* serialization *and* second serialization.

flap copy

Text on the inside portion of a book cover that usually describes the book.

foreign rights

The rights that authors give publishers to enter into contracts to publish their books in other languages and sell them abroad.

galleys

A prepublication version of a book. Galleys, which are also known as galley proofs, are typically sent to the author for review and final correction before the final version is produced.

genre

The general classification of a book such as business, parenting, writing, etc. The genre is usually indicated at the top of the back cover.

hardcover

Books bound in a stiff, protective cover that usually resists bending.

imprint

A publishing company that is a division or subsidiary of a parent company. For example, Pocket Books is an imprint of Simon & Schuster, Inc.

ISBN

The International Standard Book Number (ISBN) is a ten-digit number that identifies each title and publisher. It's used for ordering and inventory purposes.

jacket

The removable covering placed on most hardbound books that contains promotional material on the book. Also called the dust jacket.

juvenile

The term often used for children's books.

lead sentence/paragraph

The first sentence or paragraph in a piece of writing.

list

Books that a publisher has published that are still in print. A list can include books from the publisher's current season and its previous seasons.

literary agent

The representative who sells the author's work to a publisher. An agent usually negotiates the book contract and receives a percentage of the income generated by the book.

LMP

Literary Market Place (R. R. Bowker). A directory of the publishing industry that is published annually.

mail order

Sales of books by publishers directly to buyers that do not go through booksellers or other intermediaries.

manuscript

The complete version of a book that is submitted for publication.

mass market

Books sold at retail outlets other than traditional booksellers. Includes warehouse stores, department stores, newsstands, and specialty stores. For example, a store that specializes in selling games may sell a book on chess.

midlist

A book that doesn't make the bestseller list. The term is also used for authors of midlist books.

option

The right that authors grant their publishers giving them the first opportunity to acquire their next book.

out-of-print (OP)

Books that a publisher no longer prints or has in stock.

overview

The opening section of a book proposal that describes the book and its market. Also called the introduction, summary, synopsis, or vision.

packagers

Those who bring the concepts for book projects to publishers and then supervise the creation of the products that the publishers release. They frequently work with writers, designers, and others to bring their projects together.

platform

An author's following and media presence. Usually means that the author has achieved renown as a frequent speaker and/or writer, for hosting a popular Web site, for having a large list of names, or for receiving wide media coverage.

premium

Books sold in volume at a discounted price as part of a promotion.

primary rights

The basic rights that a publisher acquires from an author when it acquires the author's books. *See also* subsidiary rights.

print on demand (POD)

A process that prints only books that have been ordered. POD books can be printed one at a time as opposed to in large print runs.

proofreading

Editing of manuscripts and galleys to correct any spelling and grammar mistakes, catch typographical and typesetting errors, and review appearance of pages. This is usually done after the copyediting stage, and is performed by professional editors at the publisher's expense.

proposal

The format in which publishers require books to be submitted in order for them to consider the books for publication.

publication date

The date when a book is delivered to retailers for sale. Also referred to as the "Pub date."

Publishers Weekly (PW)

The main publication providing information to the publishing industry.

query or query letter

A written submission to agents and editors to determine if they would be interested in representing an author, publishing an author's book, or learning more about the book. Queries via e-mail have recently become more popular.

remaindered

Books that are offered for sale well below their cover prices. Usually they are books that didn't sell well or that have been around for a while.

reprint rights

The authorization to republish a book, or to publish different versions or formats of it, after its initial publication.

reserve

Funds that are not paid out to authors in order to meet a stated contingency. In publishing, amounts in reserve are held for books that the publisher estimates will be returned by booksellers.

returns

Books that haven't sold and are returned to the publisher. It's standard practice in the book-publishing industry to allow retailers and wholesalers to return books that haven't sold.

review copies

Free copies of a book that are sent, usually prior to publication, to book reviewers and other media people.

royalties

The amount that authors receive from publishers for the sales of books and subsidiary rights. Royalties are usually calculated as a percentage of the income generated by the book.

SASE

The abbreviation for "self-addressed, stamped envelope," which should be included with authors' submissions to agents and publishers if they want their submissions returned.

secondary rights

See subsidiary rights.

second serialization

The publication of selected portions of a book, usually in periodicals, after the book has been released. *See also* first serialization *and* serialization.

self-published

The term for a book that an author publishes him- or herself and not through a traditional publishing company. Typically, the authors handle, or hire others to handle, all writing, editing, design, printing, and distribution themselves. *See also* vanity publishing.

serialization

The publication of selected portions of a book in periodicals. *See also* first serialization *and* second serialization.

sidebar

Additional information included in a manuscript's text that is usually placed in a box or a shaded area or set off in another design format.

slush pile

The place where unsolicited manuscripts are placed before they are read by editors.

special sales

Book sales made to outlets other than traditional booksellers. Frequently, these sales are for a large number of books.

subagent

See coagent.

subsidiary rights

The rights to reprint, serialize, and reproduce a book for movies, television, audio and video recordings, and electronically.

textbooks

Books created for and sold to educational markets.

trade books

Books sold through traditional channels to bookstores and book clubs.

translation rights

The authority to publish a book in languages other than the language in which it was originally published.

unagented

An author or a book that is not represented by a literary agent.

unsolicited

A submission that was not requested by the recipient. Usually refers to queries, proposals, or manuscripts sent to agents, editors, and publishers.

vanity publishing

The process in which an author pays a company to publish his or her manuscript. Some vanity publishers also provide editing, design, and distribution services.

Appendix B

Resource Directory

IN CREATING THIS DIRECTORY, we have tried to include the best resources and the most up-to-date information about them. However, resources continually change: They move, merge, refocus the direction of their business, and even shut down. In addition, when you refer to this list, it may be long after we compiled it, so some information may not be current. To be on the safe side, check the resource directory on our Web site, *www.author101.com*, which should have the latest information.

> **LEGAL NOTICE:** This list is provided strictly as a resource guide and to inform you of the resources that may be available to you. Readers should independently check all information about these resources before using them. The authors and publisher specifically assume no liability for the use of this resource directory, nor do they guarantee its accuracy.

BOOK PUBLISHING

R. R. Bowker, 630 Central Avenue, New Providence, NJ 07974; Tel: (888) 269-5372. E-mail: *info@bowker.com*.
✐ *www.bowker.com*

BookMarketing.com. John Kremer's online warehouse of information on book publishing, marketing, and promotion.
✐ *www.bookmarket.com*

Information Today, Inc., Literary Market Place (LMP), 143 Old Marlton Pike, Medford, NJ 08055-8750; Tel: (800) 300-9868; Fax: (609)

654-4309. E-mail: *custserv@infotoday.com*. This directory of the publishing industry includes lists of publicists, publishers, agents, lecture agents, organizations, media, writers' conferences, trade services, and international resources.

✐ *www.literarymarketplace.com*

Para Publishing. Dan Poynter's site provides tons of information on publishing. Free documents and statistics plus books, reports, disks, and tapes.

✐ *www.parapublishing.com*

Publishers Marketplace. Electronic newsletter that tracks deals, sales, reviews, agents, editors, news. Includes Publishers Lunch Deluxe.

✐ *www.publishersmarketplace.com*

Publishers Weekly. The news magazine of the book industry that is read by most major publishers. Reports on all segments of the industry, including creation, production, marketing, and sales.

✐ *www.publishersweekly.com*

The Book Standard. Reports on the book market by giving sales figures, analyses, news, reviews, commentary, job boards, and database resources.

✐ *www.thebookstandard.com*

BOOK PROMOTION

PMA: Independent Book Publishers Association, 627 Aviation Way, Manhattan Beach, CA 90266; Tel: (310) 372-2732; Fax: (310) 374-3342. E-mail: *info@pma-online.org*. Runs the PMA Publishing University, which is usually held the two days before the annual BEA trade show begins.

✐ *www.pma-online.org*

BestSeller Mentoring, Randy Gilbert and Peggy McColl, 398 E. Eaglewood Lane, Mt. Jackson, VA 22842; Tel: (540) 856-3318. E-mail: *support@bestsellermentoring.com*. *Make Your Book an Online Best Seller.* Learn how to sell tons of books online and get onto the bestseller list for Amazon.com, Barnes & Noble, Books-a-Million, 800-CEO-READ, etc.

✎ *www.BestSellerMentoring.com*

PR Leads, Daniel Janal, P.O. Box 130, Excelsior, MN 55331; Tel: (952) 380-1554. E-mail: *dan@prleads.com*.

✎ *www.prleads.com*

PUBLICITY SERVICES

Planned TV Arts, Contact: Rick Frishman, 1110 Second Avenue, New York, NY 10022; Tel: (212) 593-5845; Fax: (212) 715-1667. E-mail: *Frishmanr@plannedtvarts.com*. PTA is one of the leading book publicity firms in the United States, specializing in radio, print, and national TV and radio placements for all authors. They work with major publishers (Random House, Simon & Schuster, Rodale, etc.) and love small publishers, too!

✎ *www.plannedtvarts.com*

Rick Frishman. You can get Rick's Million Dollar Rolodex at *www.rickfrishman.com*.

The Spizman Agency, Contact: Willy Spizman, Atlanta, GA; Tel: (770) 953-2040. E-mail: *willy@spizmanagency.com*. The Spizman Agency is a full-service public relations firm that specializes in marketing, promoting, and publicizing books, products, and leading-edge experts. They have worked with many bestselling authors and publishers as well as with first-time authors launching their books and literary careers. The Spizman Agency oversees the Think About It program at Turner Broadcasting and serves as the Atlanta affiliate of Planned Television Arts. The agency focuses on print and broadcast placement, book development, and comprehensive book consultation.

✎ *www.spizmanagency.com*

AceCo Publishers, Alex Carroll, 924 Chapel Street #D, Santa Barbara, CA 93101; Tel: 1-877-733-3888. E-mail: *Alex@RadioPublicity.com*. Web: *www.1shoppingcart.com/app/aftrack.asp?afid=29117*. *Alex Carroll's Radio Publicity Home Study Course.* The ultimate in learning how to get yourself booked on the largest radio shows.

✐ *www.RadioPublicity.com*

North American Precis Syndicate, Jim Wicht, Empire State Building, 350 Fifth Avenue, 65th Floor, New York, NY 10118; Tel: 1-800-222-5551. E-mail: *jimw@napsnet.com*. NAPS National Newspaper Feature Service. Covers 10,000 newspapers nationwide. A great way to get feature stories on your product or book published in daily and weekly newspapers throughout the country . . . at very low cost. Tell Jim that Rick Frishman sent you, to get a special bonus.

✐ *www.napsnet.com*

Metro Editorial Services, 519 Eighth Avenue, New York, NY 10018; Tel: (800) 223-1600; Tel: (212) 223-1600. E-mail: *mes@metro-email.com*. Prepares and sends a feature news story to more than 7,000 newspapers monthly. Also sends out themed material to targeted audiences.

✐ *www.metroeditorialservices.com*

PR Newswire, 810 Seventh Avenue, 35th Floor, New York, NY 10019; Tel: (212) 596-1500; Tel: (800) 832-5522. Sends news releases to targeted or all media nationally and internationally.

✐ *www.prnewswire.com*

Bradley Communications, 135 E. Plumstead Avenue, P.O. Box 1206, Lansdowne, PA 19050-8206; Tel: (610) 259-1070; Tel: (800) 784-4359; Fax: (610) 284-3704. *Radio TV Interview Report.* Sends a description of your expertise and media pitch to more than 4,000 media outlets.

✐ *www.rtir.com; www.freepublicity.com*

Pneuma Books, LLC. 327 Curtis Avenue, Suite Five, Elkton, MD 21921; Tel: (410) 996-8900; Fax: (410) 996-8901. The premier book development, design, and marketing solution for publishers; not a subsidy publisher or vanity press.

www.pneumabooks.com

Foster Covers, George Foster, book cover designer, 104 S. Second Street, Fairfield, IA 52556; Tel: (641) 472-3953; Tel: (800) 472-3953; Fax: (641) 472-3146. E-mail: *foster@lisco.com.*

www.fostercovers.com

RJ Communications, Ron Pramschufer, 51 East Forty-second Street #1202, New York, NY 10017; Tel: (800) 621-2556; Fax: (212) 681-8002. E-mail: *Ron@RJC-LLC.com.* Has thirty-plus years in the business, specializing in all areas of the design and manufacture of fiction, nonfiction, and children's picture books. Free e-mail and telephone consultation.

www.BooksJustBooks.com

Penelope Paine, 817 Vincente Way, Santa Barbara, CA 93105; Tel: (805) 569-2398. E-mail: *PPPennyP@aol.com.* Specializes in children's books and selling to school systems.

Jane Centofante, 10616 Rochester Avenue, Los Angeles, CA 90024; Tel: (310) 475-9758; Fax: (310) 474-0814. E-mail: *jfcento@aol.com.* Editor of nonfiction bestsellers; edits manuscript for content and structure so it's publisher-ready.

Media + (Media Plus), Judith Kessler, 828 Westbourne Drive, West Hollywood, CA 90069; Tel: (310) 360-6393; Fax: (310) 360-0093. E-mail: *jude001@earthlink.net.* Award-winning writer/creative consultant in all forms of media, including book proposals and media training.

Quinn's Word for Word, Robin Quinn, 10573 West Pico Boulevard #345, Los Angeles, CA 90064; Tel: (310) 838-7098; Fax: (same). E-mail: *quinnrobin@aol.com*. Copyediting, writing, proofreading, manuscript evaluation, and ghostwriting. We make your ideas sparkle.

Cypress House, Cynthia Frank, 155 Cypress Street #123, Fort Bragg, CA 95437-5401; Tel: (707) 964-9520; Fax: (707) 964-7531. E-mail: *qedpress@mcn.org*. Editing, production, and promotion services for new publishers. Personalized and reasonable.

GHOSTWRITERS

Mark Steisel, Tel: (415) 454-9161, (415) 454-0125. E-mail: *msteisel@ earthlink.net*. Rick's favorite ghostwriter.

Tim Vandehey. E-mail: *tim@pacificwhim.com*.

Word Wizard, David Kohn, 3117 Lake Shore Drive, Deerfield Beach, FL 33442; Tel: (954) 429-9373. E-mail: *WordWiz@gate.net*. Award-winning ghostwriting, editing, manuscript analysis, coaching. Twenty-five years of experience.

Mahesh Grossman, Tel: (561) 434-9044. E-mail: *getpublished@authors team.com*.

COPYRIGHT AND PUBLISHING ATTORNEYS

Lloyd Jassin, Esq., The Actors' Equity Building, 1560 Broadway #400, New York, NY 10036; Tel: (212) 354-4442; Fax: (212) 840-1124. E-mail: *Jassin@copylaw.com*.

✒ *www.copylaw.com*

Charles A. Kent, Esq., 1428 de la Vina, Santa Barbara, CA 93101. Tel: (805) 965-4561.

Law Offices of Jonathan Kirsch, 1880 Century Park East, Suite 515, Los Angeles, CA 90067; Tel: (310) 785-1200. E-mail: *jk@jonathan kirsch.com.*

Ivan Hoffman, Attorney at Law, P.O. Box 18591, Encino, CA 91416-8591; Tel: (818) 342-1762; Fax: (419) 831-2810. E-mail: *ivan@ivan hoffman.com.*
✍*www.ivanhoffman.com*

Venable, Jeff Knowles, 1201 New York Avenue NW #1000, Washington, DC 20005; Tel: (202) 926-4860. E-mail: *jdknowles@venable.com.*
✍*www.venable.com*

Joel Berman Esq., 780 Third Avenue, New York, NY 10017; Tel: (212) 583-0005. E-mail: *joel@joelsberman.com.* Every type of legal issue. Wills, estates, and if you need to sue someone.

CLIPPING SERVICES

Bacon's Clipping Bureau, 332 S. Michigan Avenue #900, Chicago, IL 60604; Tel: (312) 922-2400; Tel: (800) 621-0561; Fax: (312) 922-3127.
✍*www.bacons.com.*

BurrelleLuce Press Clipping Service, 75 E. Northfield Road, Livingston, NJ 07039; Tel: (973) 992-6600; Tel: (800) 631-1160; Fax: (973) 992-7675.
✍*www.burrellesluce.com*

BurrellesLuce Press Clippings, 589 Eighth Avenue, 16th Floor, New York, NY 10018; Tel: (212) 279-4270; Fax: (212) 279-4275.

Canadian Press Clipping Services, 2206 Eglinton Avenue E. #190, Toronto, Ontario M1L 4T5, Canada; Tel: (416) 750-2220, ext. 203.

Newsclip Clipping Bureau, 363 W. Erie Street, Chicago, IL 60610; Tel: (800) 544-8433; Fax: (312) 751-7306. E-mail: *clip363@aol.com.* ✍*www.newsclip.com*

Freebies, 1135 Eugenia Place, P.O. Box 5025, Carpenteria, CA 93014-5025;Tel: (805) 566-1225; Fax: (805) 566-0305. E-mail:*freebies@aol.com* or *freebies@earthlink.net.* Linda Cook, editor. Published five times a year with a circulation of 350,000 paid subscribers.

ONLINE BOOKSTORES

Amazon.com—*www.amazon.com*

Barnes & Noble—*www.barnesandnoble.com*

Borders—*www.borders.com* (now teamed with Amazon.com)

BOOK WHOLESALERS

Baker & Taylor—*www.btol.com*

Ingram Book Group—*www.ingrambook.com*

MEDIA DIRECTORIES

Information Today, Inc., 143 Old Marlton Pike, Medford, NJ 08055-8750; Tel: (609) 654-6266; Fax: (609) 654-4309. E-mail: *custserv@infotoday.com. Literary MarketPlace (LMP)* has lists of book reviewers and talk shows as well as publicists. The first place to check out media directories is at your library. See what they offer and how much they cost, and then decide how to get what you need. ✍*www.literarymarketplace.com*

Bacon's Information, 332 S. Michigan Avenue #900, Chicago, IL 60604; Tel: (800) 621-0561. *Bacon's Media Calendar Directory* lists the lead editorial calendars of 200 daily papers and 1,100 magazines. Important if your book's sales are keyed to a holiday. Includes a free bimonthly newsletter. ✍*www.bacons.com*

R. R. Bowker, 630 Central Avenue, New Providence, NJ 07974; Tel: (888) 269-5372; Fax: (908) 771-7704. E-mail: *info@bowker.com*. Publishes *Broadcasting & Cable Yearbook* and *Ulrich's Periodicals Directory*.
✎ *www.bowker.com*

BurrellesLuce, 75 E. Northfield Road, Livingston, NJ 07039; Tel: (973) 992-6600; Tel: (800) 631-1160; Fax: (973) 992-7675.
✎ *www.burrellesluce.com*

Adweek Directories, 1515 Broadway, New York, NY 10036.
✎ *www.adweek.com*

The Yellow Book Leadership Directories. Leadership Directories, 104 Fifth Avenue, New York, NY 10011; Tel: (212) 627-4140. Directories of media, associations, law firms. The Web site has media and industry news.
✎ *www.leadershipdirectories.com*

AceCo Publishers, Alex Carroll, 924 Chapel Street #D, Santa Barbara, CA 93101; Tel: (805) 962-7834; Fax: (805) 564-6868. E-mail: *Alex@RadioPublicity.com*. *Alex Carroll's Radio Publicity Home Study Course.* Offers a database of radio stations as well as a course on getting publicity via radio phone interviews.
✎ *www.1shoppingcart.com/app/aftrack.asp?afid=29117*

Media Distribution Services, 307 West Thirty-sixth Street, New York, NY 10018-6496; Tel: (212) 279-4800; Tel: (800) 637-3282. Has lists for all media. Will blast-fax, print, and mail.
✎ *www.mdsconnect.com*

Infocom Group, 5900 Hollis Street #L, Emeryville, CA 94608; Tel: (510) 596-9300; Tel: (800) 959-1059. E-mail: *info@infocomgroup.com*. *National PR Pitch Book* and *Bulldog Reporter's MediaBase* custom lists.
✎ *www.infocomgroup.com*

"The Tip Sheet"—Monthly newsletter by Planned TV Arts, 1110 Second Ave., New York, NY 10022; Tel: (212) 593-5820. To sign up, go to *www.plannedtvarts.com*.

Open Horizons, P.O. Box 205, Fairfield, IA 52556; Tel: (641) 472-6130; Tel: (800) 796-6130; Fax: (641) 472-1560. E-mail: *info@book market.com*. *Book Marketing Update.* A twice-monthly newsletter about promotion. Editor-in-Chief John Kremer, author of *1001 Ways to Market Your Books*. Provides marketing tips and techniques, Internet sources, and media contacts.

✍ *www.bookmarket.com*

Infocom Group, 5900 Hollis Street #L, Emeryville, CA 94608-2008; Tel: (800) 959-1059. E-mail: *Bulldog@infocomgroup.com*. *Bulldog Reporter.*

✍ *www.bulldogreporter.com*

Partyline, 35 Sutton Place, New York, NY 10022; Tel: (212) 755-3487. E-mail: *byarmon@ix.netcom.com*. New media, interview opportunities.

✍ *www.partylinepublishing.com*

Speaker Net News, 1440 Newport Avenue, San Jose, CA 95125-3329; Tel: (408) 998-7977; Fax: (408) 998-1742. E-mail: *editor@speakernetnews. com*. A free weekly newsletter aimed at speakers. Also provides valuable ideas for writers.

✍ *www.speakernetnews.com*

Ragan Communications, 316 N. Michigan Avenue, Chicago, IL 60601; Tel: (800) 878-5331. *Ragan's Media Relations Report.* Provides information on trends, media tips, and interviews.

✍ *www.ragan.com*

CONFERENCE RESOURCES

How to Build a Speaking and Writing Empire, a seminar run by author Mark Victor Hansen (of the *Chicken Soup for the Soul* series). For a brochure, call (800) 423-2314.

Literary Market Place and the May issues of *Writer's Digest* and *The Writer* magazines list writers' conferences.

ShawGuides—*www.shawguides.com/writing*

Maui Writer's Conference—*www.MauiWriters.com*

WEB SITE DESIGN AND MANAGEMENT

Rick's Cheap Domains. Get domains for $8.95.
✑ *www.rickscheapdomains.com*

Membership101. Create your own membership Web site.
✑ *www.membership101.com*

Web Solutions. Solutions for managing your Web sales and marketing.
✑ *www.rickswebsolution.com*

PlanetLink, P.O. Box 5428, Novato, CA 94948; Tel: (415) 884-2022. E-mail: *sales@planetlink.com*. Works with businesses that want an Internet game plan and a Web site that works. Web site design services, search engine promotion, hosting, and Internet consulting.
✑ *www.planetlink.com*

Phil Huff, P.O. Box 14, Mt. Pleasant, SC 29465; Tel: (843) 568-5640. E-mail: *philhuff@philhuff.com*.
✑ *www.themarketingwebmaster.com*

Artslynx International Writing Resources. Lists organizations for writers and has links to other sites.
www.artslynx.org/writing

Associated Writing Programs. Includes lists of college writing programs and writers' conferences.
www.awpwriter.org

Book Flash. Provides links to news releases and other publishing information.
www.bookflash.com

Book Talk is an archive of articles about publishing and links.
www.booktalk.com

BookWire. Click on *Publishers Weekly* for a free subscription to a daily dose of publishing news. The site also provides links to other helpful sites, including dozens of online marketing companies.
www.bookwire.com

Chip Rowe's Book of Zines. Provides info about zines and a network of zine editors.
www.zinebook.com

Cluelass. A network of mystery writers.
www.cluelass.com

C-SPAN. For information on the cable TV station's book programming, go to *www.booknotes.org*.

Frugal Fun. Shel Horowitz, the author of *Marketing Without Megabucks*, offers free monthly Frugal Marketing Tips and other helpful information.
www.frugalfun.com

Gebbie Directory. Mark Gebbie provides links and e-mail addresses that will enable you to V-mail (send video e-mail to) the media. Gebbie Press specializes in online promotion.

✐ *www.gebbieinc.com*

HTML Writers Guild hosts a network of Web authors and offers help on writing and marketing for the Web.

✐ *www.hwg.org*

The Northern California Independent Booksellers Association. Offers a free newsletter by Pat Holt, a former *San Francisco Chronicle* book review editor and publishing's I. F. Stone.

✐ *www.nciba.com*

The Onion. Provides humor breaks and, by example, wisdom about writing humor.

✐ *www.theonion.com*

Pilot Search. Lists 11,000 writing links.

✐ *www.pilot-search.com*

ProfNet. Provides a link to authors and other experts for journalists and 11,000 public relations professionals.

✐ *www.profnet.com*

Put It in Writing. Jeff Rubin puts twenty-five years of journalism experience into making newsletters as effective as possible.

✐ *www.put-it-in-writing.com*

Ralan Conley's SpecFic and Humor Webstravaganza. Has information on humor and sci-fi markets, and 600 writing links.

✐ *www.ralan.com*

ShawGuides. Provides information on writers' conferences and workshops.
☞ *www.shawguides.com/writing*

Speaker Net News. A free weekly newsletter aimed at speakers that also provides valuable ideas for writers.
☞ *www.speakernetnews.com*

Visual Horizons. Designs for "200 On-Screen/MS Word," along with help on using them.
☞ *www.visualhorizons.com*

Writer's Digest. Includes daily publishing news, information about promotion, and writers' conferences.
☞ *www.writersdigest.com*

The Writer's Toolbox has resources for novelists and journalists.
☞ *www.writers-toolbox.com*

WORKSHOPS

Besides workshops, the following organizations provide a wealth of information, online and offline, about publishing and promotion.

The Jenkins Group, Jerrold Jenkins, 400 W. Front St., Traverse City, MI 49684; Tel: (231) 933-0445; Tel: (800) 706-4636; E-mail: *jenkinsgroup @bookpublishing.com.*
☞ *www.bookpublishing.com*

Open Horizons, John Kremer, P.O. Box 205, Fairfield, IA 52556; Tel: (641) 472-6130; Tel: (800) 796-6130; Fax: (641) 472-1560. E-mail: *info@bookmarket.com.* John is the author of *1001 Ways to Market Your Book.* He also edits the *Book Marketing Update* listed above and conducts three-day Book Marketing Blast-Off Seminars.
☞ *www.bookmarket.com*

Para Publishing, Dan Poynter, P.O. Box 8206-146, Santa Barbara 93118-8206; Tel: (805) 968-7277; Tel: (800) PARAPUB; Fax: (805) 96 1379. E-mail: *info@parapublishing.com.* ✑*www.parapublishing.com*

PMA: Independent Book Publishers Association, Jan and Terry Nathan, 627 Aviation Way, Manhattan Beach, CA 90266; Tel: (310) 372-2732; Fax: (310) 374-3342. E-mail: *pmaonline@aol.com.* ✑*www.pmaonline.org*

Small Publishers Association of North America (SPAN), 1618 West Colorado Avenue, Colorado Springs, CO 80904. Tel: (719) 471-2182. ✑*www.spannet.org*

BestSeller Management Consulting, Greg Godek, 5641 La Jolla Hermosa Avenue, La Jolla, CA 92037; Tel: (858) 456-7177; Fax: (858) 456-7155. Works with two clients per year in getting them on the bestseller lists.

Cross River Publishing Consultants, Thomas Woll, 3 Holly Hill Lane, Katonah, NY 10536; Tel: (914) 232-6708; Tel: (877) 268-6708; Fax: (914) 232-6393. E-mail: *twoll@pubconsultants.com.* Author of *Publishing Profit.* Consults on general management issues, publishing economics, editorial analysis, etc. ✑*www.pubconsultants.com*

"BACK OF THE ROOM" BOOK SALES

Fred Gleeck. Tel: (800) FGLEECK. ✑*www.fredgleeck.com; www.theproductguru.com; www.selfpublishingsuccess.com; www.infoproductsseminar.com*

Media and Back of the Room Sales Training. Joel Roberts, media trainer extraordinaire. Tel: (310) 286-0631.

Book Marketing Works, 50 Lovely Street, Avon, CT 06001; Tel: (860) 675-1344; Tel: (800) 562-4357. E-mail: *info@strongbooks.com. You're on the Air,* a must-have video created by Brian Jud, in which producers for major shows discuss how to prepare for and give interviews. Comes with two companion books by Jud: *It's Show Time: How to Perform on Television & Radio* and *Perpetual Promotion: How to Contact Producers and Create Media Appearances for Book Promotion.* He offers other videocassettes and audiocassettes.

✐ *www.bookmarketingworks.com*

WRITERS' ORGANIZATIONS

For the most part, the following are national organizations. *Literary Market Place* lists many others that are statewide or regional.

The Academy of American Poets, 588 Broadway, Suite 604, New York, NY 10012; Tel: (212) 274-0343; Fax: (212) 274-9427. E-mail: *academy@dti.net.*
✐ *www.poets.org*

American Medical Writers Association, 40 W. Gude Dr., Rockville, MD 20850-1192; Tel: (301) 294-5303, Fax: (301) 294-9006.

American Society of Journalists and Authors (ASJA), 1501 Broadway, Suite 302, New York, NY 10036; Tel: (212) 997-0947; Fax: (212) 768-7414. E-mail: *asja@compuserve.com.* Has chapters around the country and an annual conference.

The Authors Guild, 31 East Twenty-eighth Street, 10th Floor, New York, NY 10016; Tel: (212) 563-5904; Fax: (212) 564-8363. E-mail: *staff@authorsguild.org.* Provides a wide range of services and publishes a newsletter for its 7,200 members.
✐ *www.authorsguild.org*

California Writers, 2214 Derby Street, Berkeley, CA 94705. Is dedicated to educating writers of all levels in crafting and marketing their writing. Has chapters throughout California.

✍ *www.calwriters.org*

Christian Writers Guild, P.O. Box 88196, Black Forest, CO 80908; Tel: (866) 495-5177 (toll free); Fax: (719) 495-5181. E-mail: *nvrohrer@spiralcomm.net.* Offers a study course and workshops.

✍ *www.christianwritersguild.com*

Dog Writers' Association of America (DWAA), 173 Union Road, Coatesville, PA 19320; Tel: (610) 384-2436; Fax: (610) 384-2471. E-mail: *dwaa@dwaa.org.* Sponsors annual competitions and monthly newsletter for writing about dogs and dog competitions.

✍ *www.dwaa.org*

Editorial Freelancers Association (EFA), 71 West Twenty-third Street, Suite 1504, New York, NY 10010; Tel: (866) 929-5400 (toll free); Fax: (212) 929-5439. A nonprofit, professional organization for self-employed workers in publishing and communications.

✍ *www.the-efa.org*

Education Writers Association, 2122 P Street, NW, Suite 201, Washington, DC 20037; Tel: (202) 452-9830. E-mail: *ewa@crosslink.net.* A professional association of education reporters and writers.

✍ *www.ewa.org*

Freelance Editorial Association, P.O. Box 38035, Cambridge, MA 02238-0835; Tel: (617) 576-8797. E-mail: *freelanc@tiac.net.*

Garden Writers of America, 10210 Leatherleaf Court, Manassas, VA 20111; Tel: (703) 257-1032, Fax: (703) 257-0213.

✍ *www.gwaa.org*

Horror Writers Association (HWA), P.O. Box 50577, Palo Alto, CA 94303. E-mail: *hwa@horror.org*.
✒ *www.horror.org*

International Association of Crime Writers, North American Branch, P.O. Box 8674, New York, NY 10116-8674; Tel. and Fax: (212) 243-8966. E-mail: *mfrisquegc@apc.org*.
✒ *www.crimewritersna.org*

National Writers Association, 10940 South Parker Road, #508, Parker, CO 80134; Tel: (303) 841-0246. Presents annual conference.
✒ *www.nationalwriters.com*

Outdoor Writers Association of America.
✒ *www.owaa.org*

Overseas Press Club of America.
✒ *www.opcofamerica.org*

PEN (Poets, Playwrights, Essayists, Novelists), 568 Broadway, Suite 401, New York, NY 10012; Tel: (212) 334-1660; Fax: (212) 334-2181. E-mail: *pen@pen.org*; Web: *www.pen.org*. Western branch: PEN Center USA, West 672 S. Lafayette Park Place, Suite 42, Los Angeles, CA 90057; Tel: (213) 365-8500; Fax: (213) 365-9616. E-mail: *pen@pen-usa-west.org*; Web: *www.pen-usa-west.org*.

Poetry Society of America, 15 Gramercy Park W., New York, NY 10003; Tel: (212) 254-9628; Tel: (800) USA-POEM. E-mail: *poetrysocy@aol.com*.
✒ *www.poetrysociety.org*

Poets & Writers, 72 Spring Street, New York, NY 10012; Tel: (212) 226-3586; E-mail: *pwsubsw.org*.
✒ *www.pw.org*

Romance Writers of America (RWA), 16000 Stuebner Airline Road, Suite 140, Spring, TX 77379; Tel: (832) 717-5200. E-mail: *info@rwanational.com.*
✍ *www.rwanational.com*

Science Fiction & Fantasy Writers of America (SFWA). E-mail: *execdir@sfwa.org.*
✍ *www.sfwa.org*

Writers League of Texas, 1501 West Fifth Street, Suite E2, Austin, TX 78703; Tel: (512) 499-8914. E-mail: *awl@writersleague.org.* Presents programs, classes, workshops, contests, and supportive services for writers.
✍ *www.writersleague.org*

OTHER ORGANIZATIONS OF INTEREST TO WRITERS

American Booksellers Association, 200 White Plains Road, Tarrytown, NY 10591; Tel: (914) 591-2665; Tel: (800) 637-0037; Fax: (914) 591-2720. E-mail: *editorial@bookweb.org.* Publishes a monthly newsletter. Allied with regional associations. Sponsors ABA Convention and Trade Exhibit, held in conjunction with BEA.
✍ *www.bookweb.org*

BookExpo America (BEA), 383 Main Avenue, Norwalk, CT 06851; Tel: (203) 840-2840; Fax: (203) 840-9614. E-mail: *inquiry@bookexpo. reedexpo.com.*
✍ *www.bookexpo.reedexpo.com*

The Library of Congress, The Center for the Book, 101 Independence Avenue SE, Washington, DC 20540-4920; Tel: (202) 707-5221. Presents exhibitions and events to stimulate interest in books and reading. Operates more than thirty affiliated state centers.
✍ *www.loc.gov/cfbook*

Friends of Libraries USA, 1420 Walnut Street, Suite 450, Philadelphia, PA 19102-4017; Tel: (215) 790-1674; Tel: (800) 936-5872; Fax: (215) 545-3821. E-mail: *folusa@folusa.org*. Supports Friends of Libraries groups around the country.

✎ *www.folusa.com*

COPYRIGHT RESOURCES

U.S. Copyright Office—*www.copyright.gov*

Copyright Clearance Center—*www.copyright.com*

Appendix C
The AAR Canon of Ethics

Reprinted with the permission of the Association of Authors' Representatives, Inc.

1. The members of the Association of Authors' Representatives, Inc., are committed to the highest standard of conduct in the performance of their professional activities. While affirming the necessity and desirability of maintaining their full individuality and freedom of action, the members pledge themselves to loyal service to their clients' business and artistic needs, and will allow no conflicts of interest that would interfere with such service. They pledge their support to the Association itself and to the principles of honorable coexistence, directness, and honesty in their relationships with their co-members. They undertake never to mislead, deceive, dupe, defraud, or victimize their clients, other members of the Association, the general public, or any person with whom they do business as a member of the Association.

2. Members shall take responsible measures to protect the security and integrity of clients' funds. Members must maintain separate bank accounts for money due their clients so that there is no commingling of clients' and members' funds. Members shall deposit funds received on behalf of clients promptly upon receipt, and shall make payments of domestic earnings due clients promptly, but in no event later than ten business days after clearance. Revenues from foreign rights over $50 shall be paid to clients within ten business days after clearance. Sums under $50 shall be paid within a reasonable time of clearance. However,

on stock and similar rights, statements of royalties and payments shall be made not later than the month following the member's receipt, each statement and payment to cover all royalties received to the 25th day of the previous calendar month. Payments for amateur rights shall be made not less frequently than every six months. A member's books of account must be open to the client at all times with respect to transactions concerning the client. If a member receives in writing a claim to funds otherwise due to a client, the member shall immediately so advise the client in writing. If the member determines that the claim is serious, and that the funds should not be remitted to the client because of the claim, the member shall proceed in accordance with the following: For a period not to exceed ninety days, the member may deposit the funds in question into a segregated interest-bearing account pending possible resolution of the dispute. No later than the expiration of that ninety-day period, if the dispute remains unresolved and the claimants do not otherwise agree with respect to the disposition of the disputed funds, the member shall take such steps as may be necessary to deposit the funds with a court of competent jurisdiction, with appropriate notice to the claimants, so that the claimants will have an opportunity to present to that court their claims to those funds. Upon so depositing the funds, the member will have complied with the member's obligations under this Canon of Ethics.

3. In addition to the compensation for agency services that is agreed upon between a member and a client, a member may, subject to the approval of the client, pass along charges incurred by the member on the client's behalf, such as copyright fees, manuscript retyping, photocopies, copies of books for use in the sale of other rights, long distance calls, special messenger fees, etc. Such charges shall be made only if the client has agreed to reimburse such expenses.

4. A member shall keep each client apprised of matters entrusted to the member and shall promptly furnish such information as the client may reasonably request.

5. Members shall not represent both buyer and seller in the same transaction. Except as provided in the next sentence, a member who represents a client in the grant of rights in any property owned or controlled by the client may not accept any compensation or other payment from the acquirer of such rights, including but not limited to so-called "packaging fees," it being understood that the member's compensation, if any, shall be derived solely from the client. Notwithstanding the foregoing, a member may accept (or participate in) a so-called "packaging fee" paid by an acquirer of television rights to a property owned or controlled by a client if the member: a) fully discloses to the client at the earliest practical time the possibility that the member may be offered such a "packaging fee" which the member may choose to accept; b) delivers to the clients at such time a copy of the Association's statement regarding packaging and packaging fees; and c) offers the client at such time the opportunity to arrange for other representation in the transaction. In no event shall the member accept (or participate in) both a packaging fee and compensation from the client with respect to the transaction. For transactions subject to Writers Guild of America (WGA) jurisdiction, the regulations of the WGA shall take precedence over the requirements of this paragraph.

6. Members may not receive a secret profit in connection with any transaction involving a client. If such profit is received, the member must promptly pay over the entire amount to the client. Members may not solicit or accept any payment or other thing of value in connection with their referral of any author to any third party for any purpose, provided that the foregoing does not apply to arrangements made with a third party in connection with the disposition of rights in the work of a client of the member.

7. Members shall treat their clients' financial affairs as private and confidential, except for information customarily disclosed to interested parties as part of the process of placing rights, as required by law, or, if agreed with the client, for other purposes.

8. The AAR believes that the practice of literary agents charging clients or potential clients for reading and evaluating literary works (including outlines, proposals, and partial or complete manuscripts) is subject to serious abuse that reflects adversely on our profession. For that reason, members may not charge clients or potential clients for reading and evaluating literary works and may not benefit, directly or indirectly, from the charging for such services by any other person or entity. The term "charge" in the previous sentence includes any request for payment other than to cover the actual cost of returning materials. Members who participate in conferences or other events where writers are charged separately for individual consultations with agents in which the writer's work is read or evaluated may not provide such consultations. The foregoing shall not prevent members from accepting honoraria and/or reimbursement of expenses for participating in such conferences or other events.

Sample Author/Agent Agreements

IF YOU ARE PRESENTED with a contract that requires you to sign over your rights, or assign a portion of your royalties, it's good practice to have an attorney review it. Even if you don't use a lawyer, educate yourself about legal issues by rereading Chapter 13. Just like publishing contracts, agency agreements are not standardized. It's not about filling in the blanks.

Read both of these sample agreements. Stop after you read each paragraph and ask yourself if you fully understand what it means. Knowledge about author/agent agreements will help you deal and communicate with agents. It will prepare you for what's involved and what you can expect. Your professionalism and preparation will also impress agents.

We would like to thank the Larsen-Pomada Literary Agency and New England Publishing Associates, Inc., for so graciously allowing us to reproduce their author/agency agreements.

The Larsen-Pomada Literary Agency Agreement

Dear Michael and Elizabeth:

While trust, friendliness, and confidence are the basis for our relationship, I have read your brochure, and I am ready to put our commitments to each other in writing:

I appoint you my sole agent to advise me and negotiate sales of all kinds for all of my literary material and its subsidiary rights in all forms and media and for all future uses throughout the world. You may appoint coagents to help you. If you say that you can't handle a property, I shall be free to do as I please with it without obligation to you.

If a potential buyer for my literary work or writing services approaches me, I will refer the buyer to you.

If an idea is mine and we do not develop it together, only I have the rights to the idea or any basic variation on it. However, if another writer approaches you with the same idea or a similar idea, you are free to represent the project.

If the idea for a project is yours, only you have the rights to the idea or any basic variation on it. You may represent a project competitive to mine, provided that we agree that it doesn't lessen your ability to represent my work.

You will pay for all expenses, which arise in selling my work except photocopying my work; mailing it abroad or on multiple submissions; buying galleys and books; and legal assistance. I must approve all expenses of more than $50 for which I will be responsible.

You may receive on my behalf all money due me from agreements signed through your efforts. This includes all sales for which negotiations begin during the term of this agreement, and all changes and extensions in those agreements, regardless of when they are made or by whom.

You are irrevocably entitled to deduct 15 percent commission on all gross income earned through your agency for my writing services. For foreign rights, you may deduct 20–30%, which includes 10 percent for your co-agents. All commissions you receive will not be returnable for any reason.

I must approve all offers and sign all agreements negotiated on my behalf. Michael Larsen/Elizabeth Pomada Literary Agents will be named as my agency in all agreements I sign on all projects that you represent.

You will remit all money and statements due me within 10 working days of receiving them.

You may respond to mail received on my behalf unless it is personal, in which case you will forward it to me promptly. I will notify you promptly if I change my phone number or address.

I realize that it may take years to sell a book, and you agree to try as long as you believe it is possible. You will notify me promptly when you can no longer help on a book. Then I may do as I wish with it without obligation to you.

If a problem arises about your efforts or our relationship, I will contact you, and we will conscientiously try to solve the problem with fairness to both of us. A problem we can't solve will be resolved with a mediator or arbitrator we choose.

You or I may end this agreement with 60 days' notice by registered mail. However, you will be entitled to receive statements and commissions on all rights on properties on which you make the initial sale, whether or not the agency represents me on the sales of these rights.

This agreement is binding on our respective personal and business heirs and assigns, and will be interpreted according to California law.

I am free to sign this agreement and will not agree to a conflicting obligation. I will sign two copies, and each of us will have one. Both of our signatures are needed to change this agreement.

We sign this agreement with the hope that it will symbolize our mutual long-term commitment to the development of my career and to sharing the rewards of this growth.

_____

Date

_____

Social Security Number

_____

My Signature

_____

For Michael Larsen/Elizabeth Pomada

_____

My Name Printed

_____

Birth date

_____

_____

_____

Address

_____

FAX

_____

How I was referred to you

_____

Home Phone

_____

Office Phone

_____

E-mail Address

_____

Web site

NEW ENGLAND PUBLISHING ASSOCIATES, INC.

Agency Agreement

MEMORANDUM OF AGREEMENT made this _____ day of _____ 2004 between:

of

hereinafter "Author," and New England Publishing Associates, Inc., of P.O. Box 5, Chester, CT 06412, hereinafter "NEPA," whereby it is mutually agreed as follows:

1. The Author hereby designates NEPA to be the exclusive agent representing all rights to the Author's book-length literary works of nonfiction and fiction, unless specifically excluded herein, in all languages throughout the world for a period of not less than six (6) months from the date of this Agreement. Said rights shall include but not be limited to volume rights, translation rights, foreign English-language rights, dramatic, film and performing rights, audio rights, software and electronic rights, serial rights, and out-of-print book rights.

2. All monies received from the sale of such rights shall be paid directly to NEPA, which shall deduct a commission of fifteen (15%) percent, except as specified in paragraph 3 below, and remit the balance to the Author within no more than thirty (30) days of receipt. No readers' fees or other charges shall be made on domestic sales with the exception of duplication of full manuscripts.*

3. Where a coagent must be employed, such as in the sale of foreign, dramatic, software, or out-of-print book rights, NEPA will receive a ten (10%) percent commission of the original amount paid to the subagent and will remit the balance of the amount paid to NEPA by the subagent to the Author as specified in paragraph 2 above. Marketing certain types

of subsidiary rights, most notably foreign rights, may require NEPA to either purchase additional copies of the Author's book from the publisher or to pay overseas courier or shipping charges. Such documented expenses incurred specifically on the Author's behalf shall be charged to the Author's account and deducted from any amounts coming due the Author from NEPA.

4. NEPA shall make its best efforts to obtain contractual offers for volume rights on the most favorable terms available and shall promptly submit any offers received to the Author for approval.

5. The Author hereby authorizes NEPA to act in his or her behalf in all matters arising out of this Agreement. However, no contract shall be binding on the Author without the Author's consent and no obligation of the Author's contained in any contract shall be binding upon or the responsibility of NEPA except as explicitly provided for in writing.

6. NEPA shall be the irrevocable agent for all rights to the Works for which it obtains one or more contracts for volume rights and shall be named as such in each contract. The provisions of singular references to Author shall be deemed to include the plural and all the obligations and rights of the Author shall be deemed joint and several unless otherwise provided in this Agreement. Unless otherwise provided for herein or by written amendment, the Agency shall divide all monies due the Author into equal parts and pay the Authors separately.

7. This Agreement shall automatically be extended in perpetuity at six-month intervals unless the Author delivers written notification of termination with proof of delivery sixty (60) days prior to the expiration date.

8. If there are multiple Authors party to this Agreement, the singular references to Author shall be deemed to include the plural and all the obligations and rights of the Author shall be deemed joint and several unless otherwise provided in this Agreement. Unless otherwise provided for

herein or by written amendment, the Agency shall divide all monies due the Author into equal parts and pay the Authors separately.

9. This Agreement shall be binding upon and shall inure to the benefit of the parties and the heirs, executors, administrators, and permitted successors and assigns of the Author and upon the lawful successors and assigns of NEPA.

10. This Agreement shall be construed in accordance with the laws of the State of Connecticut regardless of its place of execution or performance and it constitutes the complete understanding of the parties. No modification, amendment, or waiver of any provision of this Agreement shall be valid or binding unless executed in writing and signed by each of the parties whose signatures are affixed hereto.

_____

For New England Publishing Associates, Inc.   Date

_____

Author   Date   Social Security Number or Tax ID Number

*Unless otherwise agreed in writing, Author shall reimburse NEPA for photocopying proposals, sample text, and manuscripts at the rate of $.05 per page for Author's initial Work and all works of fiction. (Author shall have the option to provide the necessary copies.) Payment shall be made within 30 days of invoice.

Appendix E

Publishing Contract Checklist

Publishing agreement checklist provided courtesy of Law Offices of Lloyd J. Jassin, New York, NY.

Below are issues to consider when you draft or negotiate your next publishing agreement. Each key point deserves greater attention than is given here. While not all clauses are equally important (or negotiable), a well-drafted contract will cover all, or most, of the points outlined below.

Book Contract Checklist

   XIV. General Provisions
       1. Name/address of parties
       2. Description of work (synopsis) – Tentative title, number of words, intended audience, fiction, nonfiction, etc.

    II. Grant of Rights and Territory
       1. Is it an assignment of "all rights" or a license agreement?
       2. Term or time period (i.e., usually the life of the copyright)
       3. Geographic scope
          a) The world?
          b) Limited (e.g., United States, its possessions, and Canada)
       4. Exclusive rights granted
          a) Primary rights
          –Hardcover

-Trade paperback

-Mass market

-Direct mail

b) Secondary (subsidiary) rights

-Periodical rights

    1) First serial (i.e., prepublication excerpts)

    2) Second serial

-Book club

-Dramatic rights

-Film/TV rights

-Videocassette/audiocassette

-Radio rights

-Merchandising (commercial tie-in) rights

-New technologies

-Foreign translations rights

-British Commonwealth rights

III. Manuscript Delivery

  1. Delivery requirements

    a) When due? Is the date realistic? Time is of the essence?

    b) What format? Specify size of paper, spacing, margins, etc.

    c) What to deliver?

    -Number of manuscript copies, disks (what WP format?)

    -Index (who pays?)

    -Number of illustrations, charts, photos (who pays?)

    d) Copyright permissions and releases

    -Scope of rights (does it parallel grant of rights?)

    -Who pays?

  2. Manuscript acceptance

    a) Criteria: Satisfactory in "form and content" or at "sole discretion" of the publisher? (Note: Acceptability is often a "flashpoint" for litigation.)

    b) Termination for unsatisfactory manuscript

c) Termination for changed market conditions
d) How is notice of acceptance or dissatisfaction given?
e) Good faith duty to edit
f) Return of the author advance
-First proceeds clause
-False first proceeds clause

IV. Copyright Ownership
1. In whose name will work be registered?
2. When will work be registered? (Should be done within statutory period)
3. Joint authors and collaboration agreements
4. Work for hire
5. Reserved rights

V. Author's Representations and Warranties
1. Author sole creator
2. Not previously published; not in public domain
3. Does not infringe any copyrights
4. Does not invade right of privacy or publicity
5. Not libelous or obscene
6. No errors or omissions in any recipe, formula, or instructions
7. Limited only to material delivered by Author

VI. Indemnity and Insurance Provisions
1. Author indemnifies publisher
2. Does indemnity apply to claims and breaches?
3. Can publisher withhold legal expenses? Are they held in interest-bearing account?
4. Is author added as additional insured on publisher's insurance?
5. Does publisher have ability to settle claims without prior approval of author? If so, is there a dollar amount limitation?

VII. Publication
1. Duty to publish within [insert number] months
    a) Force majeure (acts of God)
    -Any cap on delays?
2. Advertising and promotion
3. Right to use author's approved name and likeness
4. Bound galleys/review copies
5. Style or manner of publication
    a) Title consultation or approval?
    b) Book jacket
    -Right of consultation? Approval?
    c) Changes in manuscript
6. Initial publication by specific imprint or may publisher sublicense rights?

VIII. Money Issues
1. Advance against future royalties
2. When payable? (in halves, thirds, etc.)
3. Royalties and subsidiary rights
    a) Primary rights
    -Hardcover royalties
    -Trade-paperback royalties
    -Mass-market royalties
    -E-book royalties
    -Royalty escalation(s)
    -Bestseller bonus
    -Royalty reductions
        1) Deep discount and special sales
        2) Mail-order sales
        3) Premium sales
        4) Small printing
        5) Slow moving inventory
    b) Secondary (subsidiary) rights royalty splits
    -Book club (sales from publisher's inventory vs. licensing rights)

-Serialization (first serial, second serial)
-Anthologies, selection rights
-Large-print editions
-Hardcover
-Trade paperback
-Mass market
-Foreign translation
-British Commonwealth
-Future (i.e., new) technology rights
-Is the right to intermingle with third-party content included?
-Audio rights
-Motion picture/TV
-Merchandising

4. Reasonable reserve for returns
   a) What percentage withheld?
   b) When liquidated?

5. What is royalty based on? (retail price? wholesale price? net price?)
   a) At average discount of 50%, 20% of net is same as 10% of list
   b) At average discount of 40%, 16⅔% of net is same as 10% of list
   c) At average discount of 20%, 12½% of net is the same as 10% of list
6. Recoupment of advances

IX. Accounting Statements
   1. Annual, semiannual, or quarterly statements
   2. Payment dates
   3. Cross-collateralization
   4. Audit rights

5. Limit on time to object to statements
6. Limit on time to bring legal action
7. Examination on contingency basis
8. Pass through clause for subsidiary rights income
9. Reversion of rights for failure to account (important clause with smaller houses)

X. Revised Editions
1. Frequency
2. By whom?
3. Royalty reductions if done by third party
4. Sale of revised edition treated as sale of new book?
5. Reviser/author credit

XI. Option
1. Definition of next work
2. When does option period start?
3. Definiteness of terms (i.e., is option legally enforceable?)
4. What type of option? (e.g., first look, matching, topping)

XII. Competing Works
1. How is competing work defined?
2. How long does noncompete run?
3. Any reasonable accommodations?

XIII. Out-of-Print
1. How defined?
2. Notice requirements
3. Author's right to purchase plates, film, inventory

XIV. Termination
1. What triggers reversion of rights?
   a) Failure to publish within [insert number] months of manuscript acceptance

b) Failure to account to author after due notice

c) Failure to keep book in print (see Section XIII)

2. Survival of Author's representations and warranties

3. Licenses granted prior to termination survive

XV. Miscellaneous

1. Choice of governing law

2. Mediation/arbitration clauses

3. Bankruptcy

4. Modification

5. Literary agency clause

© 2004. Lloyd J. Jassin. All Rights Reserved.

Index

A

AAR. *See* Association of Authors'
    Representatives (AAR)
Abecassis, Andree, 130, 134–35
Accounting provisions, 159
Agency clause, 156
Agent ownership interests, 160–61
Agenting process, 25–43. *See also* Finding
    agents; Queries (letters/e-mails)
    long-term approach, 20–21, 42
    matching proposals with publishers,
      34–36
    negotiations, 40–41, 48–49
    overview, 25–26
    postcontract, 41–42
    proposals, 32–34, 38
    submissions. *See* Submissions
    working together, 37
Agents
    AAR membership, 14, 15–16
    advantages of, 1–9, 46–51
    advice from, 50–51
    as advocates, 49–50
    alternatives to, 57–58
    book knowledge of, 46–47
    career management from, 49
    clout of, 46
    compensation for, 10, 12, 160
    competence questions, 56
    as confidants, 41–42
    conflicts of interest with, 21, 40–41
    contact list for, 69–70
    crooked, 57
    disadvantages of, 53–59
    dual loyalty of, 55–56
    expense charges from, 12–13, 54, 159
    finding. *See* Attracting agent interest;
      Finding agents

how they work, 7–9
increased income with, 50
lack of guarantees from, 57
negotiating skills of, 48–49
new, 131
prestige of, 51
publisher relationships, 1–9, 29–30,
    34–36, 48
publishing attorneys as, 23, 24
publishing attorneys vs., 21, 23–24
reasons for, 2–3, 45, 46–51
researching, 26–28, 61–65, 67–69,
    115–16, 123–25, 182
resources from, 47
roles/responsibilities of, 2, 8, 11–12,
    41–42, 180–81
"sales first" attitude of, 54–55
specialties of, 28–30
terminating relationship with, 163–68
timing advantages of, 48
track records of, 115–16
trouble with, 58
turn-offs for, 85–86, 169–78
understanding market, 47–48
Agreements (with agents), 152–62
    accounting provisions in, 159
    agency clause, 156
    agent compensation, 10, 12, 160
    arbitration clause, 161
    attorney review of, 155
    caution, 152
    content of, 14, 154–55
    due diligence before signing, 152
    duration of, 157
    expense charges in, 159
    funds management, 160
    other considerations, 160–61
    ownership interests and, 160–61

Agreements (with agents)—*continued*
    purpose of, 155
    samples, 219–25
    scams, 153–54
    scope of authority, 155–56
    signing, 13
    state law clause, 161
    terminating, 157–59, 163–68
    types of, 154
    written vs. handshake, 13
Agreements (with publishers)
    checklist for, 226–32
    negotiating, 40–41
    signing contracts, 41
Alexander, Jill, 30–31
Applebome, Peter, 11–12
Association of Authors' Representatives
    (AAR), 14–16
    avoiding scams and, 153–54
    Canon of Ethics, 14, 17–20, 154, 215–18
    membership, 14, 15–16
    payments through agents and, 14
    reading fees and, 16–17
Atchity, Ken, 5–6
Attorneys. *See* Publishing attorneys
Attracting agent interest, 123–32
    attending conferences, 126–28
    best approach, 123–25
    focusing on strengths, 128–30
    new agents, 131
    shared values and, 125

B

Bawarsky, Harriette, 114–15
Bloomer, Liv, 85–86, 89, 134
Book publicists, 143
Brodowsky, Pamela, 96
Bykofsky, Sheree, 96

C

Canon of Ethics (AAR), 14, 17–20, 154,
    215–18
Career management, 49

Chearney, Leanne, 142
Clark, June, 26, 34, 35, 36, 130, 135
Conflicts of interest, 21, 40–41
Contact list, for agents, 69–70
Cooper, Roger, 32, 135–36
Curtis, Richard, 6, 9, 72

D

Databases, of publishers, 34–35
Di Mona, Lisa, 97
Dystel, Jane, 97–98
Economic climate, 4–6

E

Editors. *See* Publishers
Ellis, Barbara, 98–100
E-mail inquiries. *See* Queries (letters/e-
    mails)
Erin Reel, 103–4
Expectations, clarifying, 78–79, 184
Expense charges, 12–13, 54, 159

F

Face-to-face meetings/interviews, 120–21,
    126
Finances. *See also* Royalties
    agent compensation, 10, 12, 160
    attorney rates/costs, 22
    expense charges, 12–13, 54, 159
    reading fees, 16–17
    reasonable/unreasonable charges, 12–13
Finding agents, 8, 60–80, 111–22. *See also*
    Attracting agent interest
    author Web sites and, 72–73
    checking references on, 17, 119–20
    clarifying desires and, 111–13
    clarifying expectations and, 78–79, 184
    contact list for, 69–70
    educating yourself before, 61–65
    face-to-face meetings/interviews,
        120–21, 126
    initial contacts, 25–26, 74–78. *See also*
        Queries (letters/e-mails)

interview checklist, 116–19
keeping records and, 69–71
networking and, 65–66. *See also*
   Writers' conferences
opening pitches and, 74–78
preparation overview, 60–61
proactive approach to, 113–14
readiness to submit and, 73–74, 182
researching and, 26–28, 62–65, 67–69,
   115–16, 123–25, 182
serious approach to, 114–15
specialty areas and, 28–30
submission log and, 70–71
time required for, 56
track record importance, 115–16
Focus groups, 139
Freedson, Grace, 100

G

Gastwirth, Don, 13, 23, 140–41, 154, 158
Ghostwriters, 143, 200
Glossary of publishing terms, 187–94
Greenfield, George, 100–101

J

Jassin, Lloyd, 21, 23, 148, 154, 158, 159, 160
Jody Rein, 104–5

K

Katz, Jeremy, 3
Knappman, Edward, 5, 31, 35, 85
Koster, Elaine, 102

L

Laitsch, Ronald E., 27, 71
Larsen, Michael, 32, 33–34, 36, 61, 64, 83,
   135
Lawyers. *See* Publishing attorneys
Leaving agents, 163–68
Letters of inquiry. *See* Queries (letters/
   e-mails)
Literary agents. *See* Agents
Long-term approach, 20–21, 42

M

Marson, Bonnie, 126–28
Martin, Sharlene, 38–39, 69, 85, 102–3,
   124–25, 136
Media presence, gaining, 137
Meeting agents, 120–21, 126
Miller, Peter, 1, 31, 42

N

Names list, 140
Negotiations
   advantages of agents for, 48–49
   with publishers, 40–41
Networking, 65–66
New agents, 131

P

Pairings, of authors, 141
Payments. *See* Finances
Perseverance, 130, 184–85
Pitches, to agents, 74–78
Platforms, 133–44
   agents looking for, 72
   alternatives to, 140–43
   book series instead of, 141
   building, 72, 136–40
   defined, 28, 72
   documenting success for, 139–40
   exceptions for needing, 134–36
   focus groups for, 139
   gaining media presence, 137
   giving talks for, 136–37
   importance of, 133–34
   Internet for, 137
   names list for, 140
   partners for, 138
   publishing chapters for, 138
   qualitative surveys for, 139
   Web sites for, 139
Proposals. *See also* Submissions
   matching publishers with, 34–36
   readiness to submit, 73–74, 182
   submitting, 32–34, 38

Publications, industry, 35
Publishers
    agent relationships with, 1–9, 29–30,
        34–36, 48
    agreements with, 40–41, 226–32
    big six, 4–5
    consolidation of, 4–5
    databases of, 34–35
    imprint ins/outs, 5
    interest from, 39–40
    matching proposals with, 34–36
    number of, 5
    rights of, 148
    smaller, niche, 141–42
    submissions to. *See* Submissions
Publishers Lunch, 35, 62
Publishing
    business of, 3–4
    economic climate of, 4–6
    failure rate, 6
    industry publications, 35
    industry structure, 6–7
    researching industry, 61–65
    statistics, 6
Publishing attorneys, 200–201
    advantages of, 20–21
    as agents, 23, 24
    agents vs., 21, 23–24
    rates/costs, 22
    reviewing agent agreements, 155
    selecting, 22
    working with, 23–24

Q

Qualitative surveys, 139
Queries (letters/e-mails), 30–32, 37,
    81–94
    agent turn-offs and, 85–86, 169–78
    basics of, 82–85, 183–84
    content of, 87–89, 183–84
    dos/don'ts of, 83–85
    e-mail don'ts, 92
    focusing topics in, 30–31

initial contact, 25–26, 74–78
    length of, 86–87
    overview, 81
    professional-looking letters, 84–85
    proofreading, 91–92, 184
    responses to, 92–93
    samples, 89–91, 102–3, 108–9
    sending, 92
    telephone inquiries vs., 82
    what agents/publishers look for, 30–31
    writing, 82
Queries, agent comments on, 95–109
    Barbara Ellis, 98–100
    Bob Silverstein, 107–9
    Carol Susan Roth, 105
    Elaine Koster, 102
    Erin Reel, 103–4
    George Greenfield, 100–101
    Grace Freedson, 100
    James Schiavone, 105–6
    Jane Dystel, 97–98
    Jody Rein, 104–5
    Lisa Di Mona, 97
    Pamela Brodowsky, 96
    Sharlene Martin, 102–3
    Sheree Bykofsky/Janet Rosen, 96

R

Reading fees, 16–17
Reasons, for agents, 2–3
Records
    agent contact list, 69–70
    submission log, 70–71
References, checking, 17, 119–20
Researching
    agents, 26–28, 61–65, 67–69, 115–16,
        123–25, 182
    publishing industry, 61–65
Resources, 195–214
    agency business, 61–62
    attorneys, 200–201
    "back of the room" book sales, 209
    book production consultants, 199–200

book promotion, 196–97
book publishing, 195–96
book wholesalers, 202
clipping services, 201–2
copyright resources, 214
ghostwriters, 200
media directories, 202–3
newsletters, 204
online, 206–8
online bookstores, 202
organizations (other), 213
publicity, 197–98
publishing industry, 62–65
referral sources, 17
researching agents, 61–65, 67–69, 124
video media training, 210
Web site design/management, 205
what publishers are buying, 62
workshops, 208–9
writers' conferences, 26, 66, 126, 205
writers' organizations, 210–13
Rights, 145–51
bundle of (five), 146–48
categories of, 149
copyright resources, 214
to display works, 147
to distribute work/make first
publication, 147
leaving agents and, 163–67
to make derivative works, 147
overview, 145–46
to perform works, 147
primary, 149–50
of publishers, 148
of reproduction, 147
subsidiary (secondary), 150–51
Roles/responsibilities, of agents, 2, 8,
11–12, 41–42, 180–81
Rosen, Janet, 96
Roth, Carol Susan, 105
Royalties
agent ownership interests and, 160–61
bonuses, 149

escalation clauses, 149
funds management, 160
increased, with agents, 50
payments through agents, 7, 14–16
reductions from, 149–50
rights and, 149–51, 163–64
typical schedule, 15

S
Scams, 153–54
Schiavone, James, 105–6
Self-publishing, 58–59
Series of books, 141
Silverstein, Bob, 107–9
Solow, Bonnie, 30, 42, 67, 78, 136, 173
Specialties, of agents, 28–30
Submission log, 70–71
Submissions
agents presenting, 5, 6–7, 37–39
editor interest in, 39–40
proposals, 32–34, 38
publishers accepting, 6–7
readiness for, 73–74, 182
what agents/publishers look for, 30–31

T
Telephone inquiries, 82
Terminating agent relationship, 163–68
Timing, 48
Turn-offs, agent, 85–86, 169–78

W
Web sites
author, importance of, 72–73
design/management resources, 205
developing platform with, 139
Willig, John, 3, 12, 79, 119, 134
Workshops, 208–9
Writers' conferences, 26, 66, 126–28, 205
Writers' organizations, 210–13

About the Authors

Rick Frishman, president of Planned Television Arts since 1982, is one of the most powerful and energetic publicists in the media industry. In 1993 PTA merged with Ruder Finn, where Rick serves as an executive vice-president. While supervising PTA's success, he continues to work with many of the top editors, agents, and publishers in America including Simon & Schuster, Random House, HarperCollins, and Penguin Putnam. The authors he has worked with include Stephen King, President Jimmy Carter, Mark Victor Hansen, Henry Kissinger, and Jack Canfield.

Rick is a sought-after lecturer on publishing and public relations and is a member of PRSA and the National Speakers Association. He is cohost of the weekly radio show *Taking Care of Business,* which airs on WCWP in Long Island, New York *(www.tcbradio.com).* Rick and his wife Robbi live in Long Island with their three children, Adam, Rachel, and Stephanie, and a cockapoo named Rusty.

Rick is the coauthor of *Guerrilla Marketing for Writers* and of the national bestseller *Guerrilla Publicity.* His book *Networking Magic* was released by Adams Media in 2004 and immediately went to #1 at Barnes&Noble.com.

Starting in 2006, he joins coauthor Robyn Spizman to travel the country under the banner of Author 101 University *(www.author101.com).* You can e-mail Rick at *frishmanr@plannedtvarts.com,* or call him at (212) 593-5845. Visit *www.rickfrishman.com* for his Million Dollar Rolodex.

Robyn Freedman Spizman, an award-winning author, has written dozens of inspirational and educational nonfiction books, including *Make It Memorable, The GIFTionary, The Thank You Book,* and *When Words Matter Most.* Her first work of fiction, titled *Secret Agent,* is a novel for young adults. As a seasoned media personality and consumer advocate for more than twenty-three years, she has appeared repeatedly on NBC's *Today, CNN Headline News,* and is featured regularly on the NBC's Atlanta affiliate WXIA and Star 94. A popular speaker nationally on book-writing and motivational topics, Spizman is considered one of the most dynamic how-to experts in the country. In addition to her writing, reporting, and speaking, she is the cofounder of the Spizman Agency, a highly successful public relations firm in Atlanta, Georgia, that specializes in book publicity. Robyn's Web site is *www.robynspizman.com.*

"When I first began to get serious about writing and publishing my fiction, in the early 1980s, **I devoured every issue of** *Writer's Digest*. I needed guidance on writing and how to be a professional writer. WD always offers plenty of both."
–**Barbara Kingsolver**

"I strongly recommend that you start reading *Writer's Digest* magazine, which is full of tips on both the writing process and getting published."
–**Dave Barry**

EVERY ISSUE OF *WRITER'S DIGEST* DELIVERS:

- **Technique articles** geared toward specific genres: novels, nonfiction books, romance, magazine articles, and science fiction
- **Inspirational stories** of writers who are living the dream — and how they got there
- **Tips and tricks** for kindling your creative fire
- **Insider information** on what editors and agents really want
- **Professionals' secrets** for winning queries and proposals
- **The latest and greatest markets** for print, online and e-publishing
- **And much more!**

Subscribe Now
at www.WritersDigest.com, or call 1-800-333-0133

Writer's Digest is published by F+W Publications, Inc.

Announcing the Author 101

"Get Published, Get Publicized" CONTEST!

Ready to turn that great idea into a book proposal? Send it in and you could win a publishing **contract from Adams Media** and **$20,000 worth of publicity** from Planned Television Arts and the Spizman Agency!

For complete contest rules, visit:
http://www.author101.com/contest.html